NEW TEACHER

CONFIDENTIAL

teacherEDU

Praise for New Teacher Confidential

"Being a teacher comes with a steep learning curve—this book sets new teachers up for success. A must read!"

—Sam Hammond, Teacher, past president of the Elementary Teachers' Federation of Ontario & the Canadian Teachers' Federation

"I wish I had this book when I was a new teacher!"

—Megan Balsillie, Teacher

"Hazel masterfully weaves her own lessons learned throughout this book, as she aims to help new teachers be successful."

—Vicki Houston, Director of Education

"This book is packed with helpful ideas, clear examples, and evidence-based strategies for supporting new teacher induction. Shannon Hazel provides valuable insights into how beginning teachers can create classrooms in which students are engaged and feel valued. This comprehensive resource will help teachers thrive as they enter the teaching profession."

—Dr. Jenni Donohoo, Author, Researcher, and Education Consultant

"This book will be an amazing addition to every new teacher's library."

—Amy Soucie, Secondary Teacher

"This book is packed full of practical, ready-to-implement strategies."

—Deb Demers-Hewitt, 30-Year Veteran Teacher

"A must-read for every new teacher. Start your career off right with these insights from a veteran teacher."

—Sandra Fields, Elementary Teacher

NEW TEACHER

CONFIDENTIAL

SHANNON HAZEL

Contents

Introduction

It was a crisp Friday in early November. I was twenty-four years old and had spent the day running around the Greater Toronto Area doing interviews for my first teaching position. After a three-and-a-half-hour drive, I was finally back in my hometown of Windsor, Ontario.

As I settled in for the evening at my parent's house, I received a phone call from one of the school districts I had interviewed with that day. They offered me a full-time contract position as a grade 3/4 teacher at a school in Burlington. I was ecstatic! I couldn't believe it was happening. I was going to be a teacher!

As I hung up the phone, the magnitude of accepting the position started to set in.

There was only one little problem: they wanted me to start on Monday and I was currently living in Lake Geneva, Wisconsin, coaching elite gymnastics. I had only planned to come home for a three-day visit, just to attend these interviews.

I immediately called back and explained the situation. I

asked if it was possible for me to have a few days to relocate my life? The answer was a firm no. If I wanted the position I had to start on Monday.

As I hung up the phone and envisioned everything that needed to happen by Monday morning, I felt completely overwhelmed.

Within forty-eight hours I needed to give notice to my current employer, grab what few things I had with me, move to Burlington, find a place to live, and be ready to begin my new teaching career on Monday morning.

Panicked was an understatement.

I spent that first week living in a hotel room, surviving off granola bars and Fruitopia. The second week, I went to stay with some family who lived ninety minutes away from my school, which added a three-hour drive to already long days. But at least it was a free option.

Finally, during the third week I was able to locate a condo to rent and moved in immediately. I then quickly began the process of having my things moved from Lake Geneva, Wisconsin, to my new home in Burlington, Ontario.

During that second week, Thursday evening and Friday morning were parent-teacher interviews. I had officially been a teacher for nine days and was about to hold my first set of parent-teacher interviews for students who I had just met. Thankfully, the parents were fairly understanding of the situation and realized that I hadn't had enough time with their children to comment on academic progress. They were just happy to meet me and put a face to a name. Although, they did seem a bit *too* excited for their children to have a new teacher.

I learned, inadvertently, on that first evening of interviews that the parents were the "reason" that I had this job. They had been in conversation with the school district for weeks, advocating for a new teacher for their children; with the conversation culminating in a "demand" from the parents that the teacher be replaced. I wasn't sure how I felt about this, but it did explain why I wasn't allowed a few days for moving before I began my new position. It also made me feel like there was going to be intense scrutiny of everything I did.

My goal at this point was to make it four more weeks to the holiday break. Then, I would have a few weeks off with some teaching experience under my belt, which would help me get organized and feel better prepared for the remainder of the school year. By that time, I would also have my personal belongings, be able to unpack, and feel a bit more settled.

As I look back now, I appreciate how I took all these hurdles in stride and kept moving forward (although there really wasn't another choice). I remember everything feeling very chaotic and stressful, yet continuously telling myself that I could do this, and that one day, this would just be a funny story to tell about the beginning of my teaching career–and so, there it is.

I spent every waking hour working that first year. When I was not in class with my students, I was learning the curriculum and developing lessons; teaching myself how to use assessment tools; developing rubrics; searching for mentor texts; developing IEPs, scaffolding supports, and accommodations for individual students; communicating with parents; writing report cards; running extracurricular activities; and so much more. It was exhausting.

Until you've experienced being a first-year contract teacher, there aren't enough words or ways to truly communicate to someone the all-encompassing, overwhelming nature of that experience–even if you didn't have only two days' notice!

Throughout my twenty-five years in education, I worked with many new teachers in their first few years of teaching. Each time it reminded me of my own experiences as a new teacher. While most teachers typically get their first position in the town or city that they are currently living in, it is still a steep learning curve with so many real and perceived pressures coming at you from many different directions. At the center of it all there are these young faces staring at you that compel you to show up as your best self every day and make it count.

Now I'm on a mission to help new teachers feel empowered and equipped for their career in education, to develop the relationships, resilience, and balance that are necessary to sustain a long, impactful, joyful career in education. I remember what it was like to be a new teacher, and I want to help others be successful.

I've done my best to support teachers in my schools over the years. I've helped guide them, advocate for them, and assure them that they are not alone. I've made sure they know that every teacher feels the immense sense of urgency of our chosen profession, and that it can take a toll on our family, our relationships, and our personal health if not actively managed.

Most teachers do not know how to stop giving of themselves, often having nothing left to give to their own families at the end of the day. I've found that by giving teachers permission to take care of themselves, to prioritize themselves, and to advocate for themselves and their students, they can find a better balance that will hopefully sustain them through a long, meaningful, satisfying career as an educator.

Formal teacher education programs are essential to developing foundational knowledge and, although teacher candidates engage in practice teaching placements, there really is no way to replicate the full scope of a teacher's role and responsibilities on a day-to-day basis during these placements.

There is a significant gap that exists between our teacher training programs and the realities of being a teacher in our current education systems. **This book aims to fill that gap.**

Teacher candidates are coming into classrooms that are already fully established and running like a well-oiled machine. They are not held accountable for implementing new mandates, assessment methods, resources, or initiatives. They do not normally communicate with parents. They are not expected to write report cards or hold parent-teacher interviews. At this point, they also do not feel the pressures of the government, the school district, public opinion, or contract negotiations. While these placements are imperative to their learning as a student teacher, their learning is limited to certain aspects of the role.

New Teacher: Confidential will give new teachers more insight into the inner workings of the education system and the demands placed on teachers to better prepare them for the journey ahead.

Many new teachers feel alone and unsure of themselves. They are in their classrooms hiding, hoping no one will notice everything they don't know about being a teacher. I'm here to tell them that they are not alone, we've all been there! It's okay to ask for help and seek advice from more experienced teachers. It's okay not to be doing everything at 100 percent from day one.

This book will address many of the facets of the education system and a career in education that new teachers may not have considered. It will better prepare them for the realities to come and help them to navigate the challenges ahead. This book will discuss everything from working within the public sector to best practices for communicating with parents and administrators to cultivating a work-life balance, and every-thing in between.

After reading, ***New Teacher: Confidential*** you will learn:

- How to minimize undesirable behaviors and increase student success.
- The ingredients for establishing a productive learning environment.
- Easy-to-use strategies for stress-free communication with parents.
- The dos and don'ts for fostering an effective working relationship with your administrator.

- Ways to navigate the swinging pendulum in education and avoid burnout.
- Strategies for creating balance between home and school.

If you are a new teacher reading this book, I want you to know that the education community and, more specifically, the students need you.

We need all the unique qualities that you bring to our community and our schools. We need you to show up with passion and to always remember why you became a teacher. There will be hard days, but there will also be so many rewarding experiences and lives that you will touch.

There are kids out there that need YOU, specifically, to be their teacher. On those challenging days, think of those kids. You are meant to be here. Lean on your colleagues, collaborate often, and try to find joy in every day.

LESSON #1: Find Your People

Teacher Friends and Collaboration Partners are Key to Survival

While most classrooms only have one teacher, teaching really is a team sport. One of the keys to a successful and effective career in education is to find other teachers to connect and collaborate with along the way.

Collaborations can take shape in many forms. They can be in the form of grade partners, other teachers in your school, or even educators that you connect with on social media or at conferences. There are many ways to make teaching connections that are beneficial for both you and your students.

Another opportunity for collaboration is by finding classes to partner with through collaborative global projects, as pen pals or reading buddies and so forth. We are no longer limited to the people in our immediate area. There are endless partnerships going on between teachers and classes from around the globe and finding them is way easier than you may think. Some of my personal favorite classroom collaborations are the **Global Read Aloud** and **International Dot Day.**

Global Read Aloud

The premise for the **Global Read Aloud** is that one book can connect the world. It's an opportunity for teachers and students to connect with classes around the world about the same book. Different books are selected each year, for different grade levels. It is up to you to choose which book will be the focus for your class. Once selected, there are many opportunities for you to connect with other educators teaching the same grade level who are also reading the same book. Typically, these opportunities can be found on social media using the appropriate hashtags or by joining the related social media groups.

It's up to you to determine which types of activities you'd like to engage in and how often. But it is important to note that you must follow the outlined reading schedule if you plan to connect with other classes. All students need to be at the same point in the book to make authentic connections, without being either unprepared or spoiling what's to come for another class.

I enjoy having my students blog about each chapter and connecting with other classes through reading and responding to each other's blog posts. We typically culminate each week's reading by joining a virtual meetup with another class to discuss the book, as well as learn about where they live, their daily life, and their culture.

The **Global Read Aloud** is a great opportunity for authentic, cross-curricular learning. For more information or to sign up to participate, you can visit www.theglobalreadaloud.com.

International Dot Day

Similarly, **International Dot Day** is celebrated each year on September 15th. This is a great beginning of the year activity to kick off connecting and collaborating with other classes. This day stems from author Peter H. Reynolds' best-selling book, *The Dot*, which encourages readers to "make their mark."

This book can be an excellent springboard for conversations around confidence, courage, and self-discovery. It is a platform for celebrating the unique talents and gifts of each of your students and encouraging them to share their gifts with the world. The lead up to **International Dot Day** is a great opportunity for building classroom community, developing your students' mindset, and setting the tone for the school year to come.

And, of course, there are many "dot" related ways to celebrate the actual day on September 15th, from dressing in polka dots, to visual art activities, centers, or even with treats that look like dots. The ideas are endless. If you are looking for ideas, I would suggest searching hashtags on social media from previous years. You can also find more information about **International Dot Day** and learn about opportunities for collaboration at www.internationaldotday.org.

Classroom collaborations are just one of the ways available for teachers to connect. Let's have a look at some others.

Mentors

If you are a new teacher, school districts will typically have some form of an either informal or formal mentorship program. In most cases, experienced teachers have signed on to be a mentor. They are invested in showing you the ropes, answering your questions, and helping you navigate the education landscape.

If you are lucky enough to have a mentor, make good use of your time with them. To do that, I would suggest having an initial conversation about their availability as well as when and how they prefer to be reached. Being respectful of their time will help you establish an effective working relationship.

Throughout the year, keep conversations with your mentor to bigger items. If you can ask someone else a question or for guidance, do it. Save the time with your mentor for building the fundamental skills or knowledge that you need to be successful and effective as a teacher. Also remember to genuinely communicate your appreciation for their time and efforts in supporting you along the way.

Grade Partners

Same grade teaching partners may be your most valuable human asset. Whether you're new to teaching, teaching a grade that is new to you, or are transitioning into a new school, your same grade teaching partner may become your new best friend.

"What if we don't get along?"

"What if we like to do things differently?"

"What if I'm the one doing all the work?"

Yes, I get it. Sometimes the match is not ideal. However, I would encourage you to work hard to find common ground and develop a professional relationship that serves you both, and ultimately the students you teach.

A grade partner doesn't need to be a best friend. It is possible to create a positive working relationship without necessarily having a personal one. And, who knows, maybe if you hit your groove professionally, the personal friendship will come.

Working with a grade partner does not mean you need to do everything the same way, either. For example, you could collaborate on a unit plan, but then add your own style or flair to it. The goal with a grade partner is to work smarter, not harder.

11 Tasks You Could Share with a Grade Partner to Immediately Reduce Your Workload

1. Photocopying
2. Laminating
3. Lesson / course planning
4. Field trip planning
5. Creating classroom newsletters or calendars
6. Selecting mentor texts
7. Ordering books, supplies or resources
8. Creating learning centers
9. Making labels
10. Planning and preparing for student concerts or performances
11. Developing report card comments

For each of these tasks you will need to agree on the logistics. Who is doing what and when? You could either alternate the tasks back and forth or even delegate according to preference.

Different Grade Level or Specialist Teachers

Once you've been at a school for a while, you will begin to learn the strengths, preferences, and interests of your colleagues. Being part of a staff where there seems to be this unwritten agreement between everyone to use their personal strengths for the benefit of all teachers, is truly amazing. You will know you're among a staff like this when you can ask anyone to point you to a person who could help with (fill in the blank) and everyone will tell you to go to the same person. Whether you need tech help, song ideas for the school concert, book recommendations for your students, new games for gym class, or advice for supporting a struggling student–everyone points you in the same direction. Having a school community that you can turn to as things arise is priceless. If you have the pleasure of working on a staff like this, count your blessings and never take it for granted. And remember to make sure you offer your own gifts to your colleagues, as well.

Other Education Workers in Your School

Schools are busy places, full of many other education workers beyond teachers. Most schools have office staff, custodial staff, administrators, educational support workers, and maybe even school psychologists, speech-language pathologists, and social workers, among other special service providers.

> Each person in your school building, no matter the position, is a potential partner in your role as an educator.

Each person in your school building, no matter the position, is a potential partner in your role as an educator. Each of these people can play a role in helping you meet the needs of your students. Your job is to understand *how and when* to invite them to the table. If you aren't sure, I would suggest that you ask them directly.

In 2018, I took on a new teaching role in special education as a learning support teacher. The learning curve was steep and the crew of professionals I met in my new role was overwhelming. Trying to keep track of everyone that came into our building on a regular basis was challenging.

Finally, I decided that I needed to get it straight in my head who they were, why they were here, how they helped students in our school, and how they could help me in my new role as a learning support teacher.

So, one by one, I engaged each of them in a conversation as they returned to our school for their regular visits. I was astonished at the number of ways that they were able to support both teachers and students. We had these amazing human resources available to us as classroom teachers, not just for our students.

Once you understand the scope of what other educational professionals do within your school or district, you can leverage their knowledge and skills to save yourself valuable time and meet the needs of kids sooner and more effectively.

Your school may also be fortunate to have educational assistants, child and youth workers, developmental services workers, and so on supporting students daily throughout the school. These professionals are an invaluable resource for helping you determine how best to support student behavior. Pick their brains when you are trying to figure out how to navigate a new situation or need suggestions for strategies when the old ones have stopped working. They can also help scaffold learning opportunities for students with Individual Education Plans (IEPs).

And then, of course, there's office and custodial staff. If you've spent any time in a school environment, you will know that office and custodial staff are your ride or die. You will look to them often and depend on them regularly in your role as a teacher for a variety of reasons.

Teacher Friends

No one understands your daily life better than teacher friends. They are in the trenches with you and understand your daily challenges and successes as an educator in balancing the demands of your professional and personal life.

Teacher friends can provide a great listening ear, empathy, or support, and can validate your feelings when facing professional challenges. They can offer strategies and advice because they've often experienced similar situations.

Teacher friends can also be the perfect people to celebrate your professional victories with, both big and small. They can appreciate the time and effort it takes to move a struggling student forward in their learning, or to finally connect with a student who's been closed off, to have a tough parent say thank you, or to be given a leadership opportunity. It is equally important to seek them out during times of success or accomplishment and not only during challenges.

Community Partners

Whether you work in a small town or a large city, I would encourage you to spend some time developing partnerships within your community or neighborhood. These partnerships offer another layer of authentic experiences for both you and your students. They are also a great avenue for helping your students learn about the value of giving back, volunteerism, and being a good citizen.

Nonprofit Organizations

In most communities, there will be organizations that spearhead opportunities to give back through food, toy, or clothing drives, or by making monetary donations, among other options. As a class activity, you could research the organizations in your community, learn about what they do and who they serve, and then decide which groups to support. Even if you're only able to support one organization, the activity will serve to build awareness about these organizations with your students. Engagement in these opportunities also helps build classroom community as your students work together toward a common goal.

Local Businesses

Another way to engage with community partners is through experiential learning opportunities. Look for businesses in your area that are open to having your class visit and learn about their industry. Perhaps a local pizza place will have your class in to make pizzas, or a local manufacturing business will show your students how their products are made. There are a variety of ways to connect experiential learning to curriculum.

Our local grocery store hosts field trips for students at no cost. They take them through the store and explain how the different sections are organized, show them what is available, talk about reading labels, and teach them how to determine the price of items. This is a life skill that students will eventually need, and it helps bring awareness to the cost of food items, label reading, and nutrition.

You might also be able to find community partners that will support your classroom with a donation. Seasonal businesses such as apple orchards, pumpkin patches, or greenhouses may donate a class set of their goods. Local bakeries, coffee shops, or restaurants may donate food or drinks for an open house or parent night. Get creative, there are endless opportunities for your local businesses to support your school or classroom. Reach out and make a connection. They, too, are often looking for opportunities to give back and support their local community.

Municipal Events

Local municipalities typically host many events throughout the year, especially for significant dates or holidays, and often welcome participation from local schools. These are perfect opportunities for your students to make curriculum-based connections and participate in community events.

Your students can also learn more about the community they live in by visiting local landmarks, historical sites, or museums.

One of the most profound opportunities I had with my students was when we partnered with the Black History Museum. They were looking for a class to interview prominent members of the local Black community and create scrapbooks for each person that illustrated their life story. They wanted to include these scrapbooks in their museum for Black History Month.

My students were each assigned to a community member who they first interviewed, and then partnered with, to create a scrapbook of their life story for others to enjoy. The members of the Black community supplied us with pictures from significant points in their lives that they wanted to have included in their scrapbook.

This was an amazing personal experience for my students, and it provided an authentic learning opportunity that tied nicely to the curriculum as well. They also learned a great deal about the history of our local Black community. My students were so proud to return to the museum once their scrapbooks were on display and share their contributions with their own families.

In whichever way you decide to connect with your local community, remember to always have your students show appreciation. Community partners love to display notes, plaques, thank you signs, and student cards for others to see how they are supporting local schools in the area. Ideally, you want to establish partnerships that are mutually beneficial and can become a yearly collaboration.

TEACHER TIP

Always include your students in thanking community partners by creating some token of appreciation that can be displayed in their local establishment.

Final Thoughts

Whichever ways you choose to collaborate with others is up to you. The opportunities are there, but it is up to you to decide when, how, and with whom you will develop these relationships. Whether they be mentors, grade partners, other education workers, or community partners, I would encourage you to prioritize building these relationships. Leveraging the skills, interests, and resources of others will contribute to increased authentic learning opportunities for your students and, hopefully, offer you support personally as well as lessen your workload professionally.

ACTION STEPS

Here are some ways to get started with finding your people and collaboration partners:

- Ask your principal if your school district has a mentorship program for new teachers and, if so, sign up.

- Do your part to develop a collaborative professional relationship with your grade partners and/or other teachers and education professionals in your school.

- Find out what special support services are available in your school or district and learn how they can help you as a classroom teacher.

- Willingly share your areas of interest or expertise with other staff members.

- Make a list of potential local community partners and determine which may be a good fit for you and your students.

- Explore ways that your class can give back to your local community or participate in community events.

LESSON #2: Your Classroom Can Run Itself

Utilizing Structure, Routines, and Organization to Create a Productive Learning Environment

Teachers make hundreds of little decisions throughout the course of each school day. Given there are five days in a school week, and roughly 190 or so school days per year, that is a lot of decisions. I think most educators would agree that they become mentally exhausted well before they become physically exhausted.

An effective way to combat that mental exhaustion is by creating a classroom environment that is, essentially, set up to run itself. Let me explain.

When a classroom is well-organized with systems, structures, and routines in place, it is much easier to teach students to be self-sufficient and independent, thus reducing the number of questions or decisions a teacher needs to make every day. When students automatically know what to do when they have finished their schoolwork, come in from lunch, or where to put classroom items, it allows our teacher brain to focus on more important matters.

Creating flow in your classroom and setting children up to be independent enables you to focus on the learning that is happening in your classroom throughout the school day. It is also essential to creating time for small group instruction or working one-on-one with students as needed.

The Physical Environment

Start by looking at the physical environment–your classroom–and begin with decluttering. Get rid of everything that you don't need or that doesn't need to be in there. Teachers are notorious for keeping things that they might need "one day." Trust me, with the way things constantly change in education, you will probably never use most of these things again. So, start purging.

> ## TEACHER TIP
> Declutter, declutter, declutter your classroom! It will immediately create a calmer learning environment for both you and your students.

Once your classroom has only the necessities left in it, think about how you want your classroom to look, feel, sound, and flow. Things to consider:

- The age of the students, the class size, and whether any of your students have special needs that need to be considered.
- Your teaching preferences (do you prefer to stand, sit, move around, use technology, write

on a white board, have a teacher desk, and so forth).

- Will your students sit at desks or at tables? Individually or in groups?
- Will you need a carpet?
- Will you regularly use centers, technology, or need room for toys?
- Do you want a reading nook, sensory area, calming zone, or any other spot for a defined purpose?
- How much space will you need for teacher items versus student items?
- Will you post a timetable or visual schedule?
- Where will you work with individual students or small groups?
- What will your students do when they have finished their schoolwork or have free time?
- What will you use the wall space for?

Once you've given some intentional thought to how your classroom will ideally look, feel, sound, and flow, begin mapping out the essential elements. Remember to consider "flow" when deciding where to locate things or how furniture and shelves will be organized. For example, if students will be bringing their lunches into the classroom in the morning and putting them on a shelf, it makes sense to have that shelf near the door.

Classroom Seating and Learning Areas

Start by determining where and how students will engage in the learning process. Where will they sit during lessons? What seating options will be available for working on academic tasks? Will they partner or work in small groups often?

Where will you work with students? Do you prefer traditional seating, or will you have alternative seating options available?

Physical set up and seating options are essential when determining how you would like your classroom to run. If you encourage lots of group work, it doesn't make sense to have desks separated and lined up in rows. If you think that the best learning happens when the students are all gathered in front of you, then you want to ensure that you make space for bringing them closer together. Set the physical furniture up to align with your vision for your learning environment.

Personally, I like having my students' desks lined up along the outside wall of my classroom (when age appropriate) facing the wall. I've used this set up with grade three, four, and five students. This works well because I rarely require my students to sit at their desks. I prefer to have a collaborative classroom environment with differentiated seating options such as a carpet area, exercise balls, wobble stools, benches, or beach chairs. Of course, students are free to sit at their desks at any time if that is their preferred seating choice.

I find that having the desks facing the wall is also great for students who are easily distracted because they like not being able to see what is happening with the other students around them. This arrangement also gives each child some wall space to post things that are helpful to their learning, such as their schedule, math formulas or procedures, editing codes for writing, or upcoming dates.

Classroom Nooks

There are many ways to create little nooks for a specific purpose in your classroom. These spaces have a defined purpose with materials that are for use within this space. Students understand why the space is there, what it can be used for, and when it is appropriate to use it. Let's have a look at two of the more common classroom spaces.

Reading Area

Many teachers choose to have a designated reading area in their classroom, organized with a variety of age-appropriate books and other reading materials (in print, online, and in audio formats when possible). This is a great way to encourage students to read for enjoyment and not just for school purposes. By creating an inviting space, students will be drawn to want to utilize it.

Books can be expensive, and often, if you choose to purchase a classroom library students will become bored with the book choices after a few weeks. I would suggest changing out the books monthly by borrowing books from your school library. By doing so, you will be providing your students with fresh choices regularly, and you can also include books that are currently in alignment with the curriculum. A good mixture of high interest books and books related to curriculum topics is a great way to go.

Beyond the books, you could add alternative seating, cushions, book posters, or a reading lamp to set the stage for a cozy reading area. It does not need to be over the top or expensive. Often, I would bring things in from home that we no longer needed as my own kids got older.

> ## TEACHER TIP
>
> If you are looking for specific items for your classroom, let family or friends know. Your classroom can often benefit from gently used items others are giving away. Just remember to be specific, and maybe even ask them to send you a picture of the item before agreeing to take it. Otherwise, you'll find yourself needing to declutter again.

Self-Regulation Space

Often when students need time to self-regulate, they are encouraged to leave the classroom to do so. Over the course of a school year, these students will inevitably miss a significant amount of learning time. An alternative might be having a space in your classroom for students to self-regulate as needed. While there may still be times when leaving the classroom is necessary, it at least provides an opportunity first within the classroom, which will hopefully be sufficient most of the time. It also lets other students know that this is a normal life process that is encouraged. This opportunity is always available in the classroom should any student feel they need it.

A self-regulation space could have various names and encompass being used for a variety of purposes, such as a calming area for students with sensory sensitivities, a break area for students that require down time between academic tasks, a quiet space for students when their emotions are elevated, and so forth.

Again, it is important to have a designated space with tools available that work for your students. You could include posters with steps for regulating your emotions or controlling your breathing, fidget tools, music, and noise-canceling headphones, to name a few. You could also consider using a timer. Most students respond well to this strategy when they get a voice in the amount of time they are permitted. It is important to consider the needs of the student, age, and frequency when determining an appropriate time frame.

There are many other spaces you could consider including in your classroom. Take some time to consider your cohort of students and then brainstorm ideas from there that might meet their needs. You only have so much room, so you'll need to prioritize the best use of your classroom space.

Classroom Decor and Wall Space

When deciding on how to use the wall and board space in your classroom, you'll want to consider the grade and age of the students as well as functionality. Wall space is prime real estate for:

1. Posting learning support materials such as learning goals, anchor charts, sound walls, or math formulas.
2. Showcasing student learning.
3. Creating a welcoming environment for students with positive messaging.

I would recommend having a nice mix of all three elements in your classroom.

While it is nice to have pretty bulletin boards with cute themes, I would suggest keeping them to a minimum. Lean more toward displays that are student-created, encourage classroom community and shared values and, that allow your students to see themselves represented in the space.

> Resist the urge to start the school year
> with your walls completely decorated with
> purchased materials.

Resist the urge to start the school year with your walls completely decorated with purchased materials. Instead, purposefully create spaces that you will work to fill within the first few weeks with your students, or even set aside areas that will be added to throughout the year as their learning progresses.

Ideas to Get You Started with Your Wall Space

- Anchor charts
- Sound or word walls
- Learning goals and success criteria
- Student work or examples of levels of achievement

- Pictures of your students, if allowable in your district (learning, playing sports, on field trips, etc.)
- Items related to your current content areas
- Positive messages about shared values, community, a learning mindset, etc.
- Class schedules or timetables
- School or community information relevant to your students and their families

Essentially, the more personal the space is to you and your students the better. I would be remiss not to mention classroom or school rules, as well. I intentionally didn't include them in the suggested ideas because I am not a fan of having "rules" posted. To me, rules sound punitive. Instead, set expectations for students through what you allow and what you do not, and by remaining consistent in drawing attention to and encouraging the behaviors you want to see. When necessary, have a class discussion to review your expectations, highlighting the reasons why these are the expected behaviors. When students understand the reason for the expectations, they are more likely to align with them than if there is a list of rules posted on the wall.

Remember also that every available space does not need to be covered. Intentionally leaving some white space avoids making the classroom feel over-cluttered and allows for the important elements to be the focus.

Developing Flow

Flow is the most vital aspect for creating a productive learning environment that also encourages student independence.

Classrooms need to be spaces that make sense and appeal to our general nature of how things are done, especially when considering classroom routines. Before setting up your physical space, consider the following:

1. What things will students do every day?

This is the most important consideration when determining flow. Tasks such as entering and leaving the classroom; handing in schoolwork, books, or assignments; eating lunch; working in a small group with you; accessing classroom materials; sharpening pencils; and so forth.

These types of tasks deserve careful consideration and need to be set up for optimal flow with the goal being to create the most logical, easiest, least interruptive way for students to do these things day in and day out.

2. What classroom materials will students need access to daily?

Any materials that students may need to use daily need to be placed in easily accessible areas that allow for students to independently access them when needed with minimal interruption to the classroom learning environment. Items such as pencils, markers, scissors, reading materials, math manipulatives, technology, and textbooks should be clearly labelled, and students should know how to access them.

Take some time to imagine your classroom up and running. How do you want it to run? How do you want it to feel? What makes the most sense in terms of flow and student independence?

People are creatures of habit, so developing good classroom habits early helps to establish a productive learning environment by reducing unnecessary questions, movement, and interruptions.

Classroom Organization, Systems and Routines

Establishing clear and effective classroom systems and routines are the bread and butter of a high-functioning learning environment. An organized environment reduces stress and clutter and frees both the teacher's and students' minds to focus on the more important tasks at hand.

Your classroom organization, systems, and routines should

clearly communicate *'this is how we do things'* in our classroom to an outsider.

Nowhere is this more apparent than in a kindergarten classroom. I spent a few years, mid-career, in the role of teacher-librarian. For two periods each week, I covered the preparation time of one of our kindergarten teachers. It took less than one day for me to be schooled by four- and five-year-olds on *how they do things* in their classroom.

It started when I went to join them, already seated on the carpet. I went to sit in a chair that was in front of the carpet facing the students. Before my butt hit the chair, one of the students piped up and stated that that was not the teacher's chair, pointing and telling me that I needed to go sit *over there*.

Even our smallest learners thrive on routines, systems, and organization. While we may think that our oldest learners like more freedom, the opposite is true. There is a certain level of comfort that routines and predictability bring to people at any age–even as teachers.

Probably the most widely-used and most effective organizational tools for teachers are bins, baskets, shelving, and labels. There is a reason why, in August, it's hard to find baskets and bins at your local dollar store, as teachers everywhere are preparing for a new school year and organizing their classrooms.

Organizational Tips for Your Classroom

- Create distinct spaces for teacher materials and student materials
- Use baskets, bins, and shelving strategically to house materials (and then teach your students that everything in the classroom has its proper place)
- Create labels for everything from book bins to locker assignments to student notebooks
- Use lower shelving for student materials and higher shelving for teacher materials

- Color code student notebooks (math notebooks are all blue, science notebooks are all green, etc.)
- Post a timetable or visual schedule
- Create a space for charging technology (dish racks are a cheap option)
- Create a designated space for students to hand in their schoolwork

Once your classroom is well organized, you'll have a great foundation for developing your classroom systems and routines.

For even the smallest routines, a little bit of forethought will be a sanity saver once your classroom is in full swing. Do your best to think through all aspects of how you want your classroom to run. However, you should know that there will be things along the way that you either hadn't considered or that need to be tweaked, and that's okay. Even the best laid plans sometimes need an adjustment.

Opportunities for Implementing Systems and Routines

- Morning entry and dismissal
- Indoor and outdoor lunch time or recess
- Bathroom breaks
- Handing in agendas, schoolwork, parent notes, or forms
- Homework
- Gaining your attention or signaling they need help
- Small group or individual instruction time
- Independent work, partnering, or group work
- Activities for when students have completed school tasks
- Accessing classroom materials
- When substitute teachers are in your room
- In the gym, library, music room, or any other learning space your students visit

- During assessments
- When using technology

Morning entry is arguably the most crucial time to have a well-established routine that students follow in the same manner every day. It is quite busy when students are making the transition from home into school, bringing with them homework, parent notes, lunches, and so forth, and adjusting to a new school day.

It is also the time where you are first greeting them, setting the tone for the day, and on the lookout for students that may not seem school-ready. In many schools, morning entry is usually followed with some type of school-wide morning announcements that will require order and attention from both staff and students. Lots of important things happen in the first few minutes of every school day.

Entry routines can often look like a checklist of must-dos that may go something like this:

Sample Morning Entry Routine

Students enter the school building and immediately place their outdoor wear and backpacks in their locker or coat room and remove the items that need to be brought into the classroom. Upon entering the classroom, they hand in homework, agendas, parent notes, and so forth by placing them in clearly labeled baskets accordingly. They then find their seat and begin with a transitional task such as reading, a quick write, or an "eye-opener" type question while waiting for morning announcements to begin.

Most well-run classrooms have some version of this morning routine happening every day. When students know exactly what is expected of them, and it is consistently expected in the same manner every day, it will become habit. Creating routines that turn into habits is the foundation of a productive classroom environment.

> Creating routines that turn into habits is the foundation of a productive classroom environment.

You will know you are in an organized classroom with clear systems and routines the moment you enter one. If you were to stand at the door and observe, you might notice:

- All students are actively engaged in a task (not necessarily the same task)
- The teacher is free to work with students as needed
- Students can independently access what they need when they need it
- Students know what to do and when without asking for direction
- It feels, looks, and sounds calm
- There is evidence of the current learning goals

In these classrooms, a different teacher could step in for the day and the classroom would continue to function in the same manner. These classrooms are a dream for a substitute or occasional teacher.

Visual Schedule and Timetables

Posting a visual schedule or timetable is necessary for some students, but good for all. Having it posted allows all students to know what to expect from their day and helps them to mentally prepare for what's to come. It also helps students stay organized and keep track of their schoolwork.

For some students, visual schedules or timetables can be key to their ability to function and successfully navigate their school day. This is especially so for students who might lack adaptive skills, struggle with cognitive flexibility, or feel anxious at school. For these students, a posted schedule can minimize emotional outbursts or undesirable behaviors that stem from these cognitive deficits.

Post your visual schedule or timetable in the format that works best for your students and is age appropriate. Then, consider whether individual students would benefit from having a more personalized option available to them and create or modify these, as necessary. Some might also benefit from having it on their desk or in their binder.

You can also make your timetable available to parents. Parents can use it to help keep their child organized with schoolwork and as a springboard for conversations about their learning each day.

The First Two Weeks

The first two weeks of school are pivotal for connecting and developing relationships with students, establishing classroom norms and culture, and teaching students about classroom organization, routines, and expectations.

During these first two weeks, curriculum comes secondary to cultivating a productive, functional learning environment and establishing classroom community.

That's not to say that learning isn't happening, but rather that the focus is on these other aspects for the moment. From a curriculum standpoint, the first two weeks of school are a critical time for diagnostic tasks and determining where your students' skill levels are currently.

This can be accomplished by developing academic tasks for your students that are focused on building classroom community while providing an opportunity for students to demonstrate their current skills.

Following are three examples of classroom community-building activities that also allow you to learn about your students' skills.

1 *Building a Community Web*

Grab a ball of yarn and have your students sit or stand in a circle. Start by sharing something about yourself and then toss the ball of yarn to a student, while still holding on to the end of the yarn. The student that catches the ball of yarn then shares something about themself and, still holding on to a piece of the yarn, tosses the ball to a classmate. This continues until all students have had the opportunity to participate.

It's important to note that, whenever you engage in a classroom activity of this nature, students should always have the option to pass. Never force students to come up with an answer. The goal of the activity is to build community, not to embarrass students. To develop a true community of learners, non-participation always needs to be a safe option for students.

This activity is open-ended and allows you to take the conversation in any direction. You could ask students to share a random fact about themself, name their favorite subject, share what they don't like about school, or even just their favorite color–something that is age appropriate. The point of the activity is to learn more about who is comfortable speaking in front of the class, who is a risk-taker, who passes and why, who gives one-word answers, and who could go on for days talking about themself.

This is all useful information to know as you begin to get to know your students and develop a connection with them. It also gives you some insight into their communication skills. Most importantly, at the end of the activity you will have created a visual showing how all of you are connected as a community of learners.

This is a perfect opportunity, while everyone is holding on to their piece of yarn which visually shows the connection between them, to have a conversation about the classroom culture and community you would like to see during the school year.

2 Top Ten Lists

To get to know your students, and more importantly to know what matters to them, you could ask your students to write a list of the most important things they want you to know about them. Begin by giving them some examples and brainstorming ideas together to get them started on the right track. The goal is to pull meaningful information out of them, not get a list of their favorite color, food, song, and so on.

You could even consider sharing your own top ten list first to allow your students to get to know you a bit better and see where they naturally make connections with you.

Prior to handing them in, you could even have your students share their top ten list with a partner, small group, or read it to the entire class.

This simple activity will give you good insight into their reading and writing skills, while allowing you to learn a great deal about them personally. This is also great information to keep in your back pocket for later when you're looking for a way to connect individually with students.

3 Back-to-School Shopping

In groups, give your students a fictitious budget to "purchase" back-to-school supplies (either for your classroom as a whole or for their individual group). For younger students, you could provide a list of items with prices to choose from. Older students could use technology to research the school supplies online, noting what they would buy and from where.

Once the exercise is complete, you could have each group share with the class what they purchased and the costs associated, as well as explain why they chose those items. What was their thinking behind what they chose to buy?

An activity of this sort provides lots of valuable information for you as the teacher. Firstly, it allows you to quickly learn about how each of your students functions as part of a group. Who are the leaders, the cooperators, the problem solvers, the organizers, and so forth? Who requires some encouragement to get involved or struggles to assume a role in the group? Who is kind and inclusive? Doing group activities during the first few weeks of school will allow you to make an informed decision about how you see group work fitting into your classroom learning environment.

Secondly, it provides an opportunity to observe your students' research, communication, and technology skills, as well as functional reading, writing, and math skills.

These are just three of many community-building activities that you could use with your students to get to know more about them personally as well as assess their current level of academic skills.

Final Thoughts

Spend the necessary time before the start of the school year to purposefully design and create your classroom environment. It will free up hours of your time throughout the school year, provide students with a welcoming environment conducive to learning, and minimize unnecessary stressors during the school day. It is time well spent.

Similarly, by using the first few weeks of school for building community and getting to know your students, both personally and academically, you will begin to establish a learning community while building genuine connections with your students. You will also glean helpful information about your students' current academic strengths and needs.

When done well, you will then be able to hit the ground running with curriculum.

ACTION STEPS

Here are some suggestions for preparing your classroom to be a well-run, organized, productive learning environment:

- Set a vision for how you would like your classroom to look, feel, sound, and flow.
- Declutter, declutter, declutter your classroom.
- Read individual student documentation or reports and determine where considerations need to be made.
- Map out your physical environment, including wall space, on paper in a way that makes sense for you before arranging and organizing the physical environment.
- Put a call out to family and friends for items that you need for your classroom (be specific).
- Borrow books from the school library to use in your classroom library.
- Create a large timetable or visual schedule to post in your classroom, as well as an electronic or paper version to share with parents; modify for individual students, as necessary.
- Intentionally plan out the first two weeks of school to focus on getting to know your students, building classroom community, and assessing current skill levels.

LESSON #3: Kids Don't Learn from Teachers They Don't Like

Connecting with Students Is the Best Classroom Management Strategy

I began my teaching career at an affluent school. The students in my class had every opportunity available to them. They had solid home lives, support with homework assignments, and two parents who showed up for parent-teacher interviews and school events.

Although the daily communication expectation from many parents was time consuming, it was amazing to have them completely involved in supporting their children's learning at school. It really did make my job easier as an educator. Yet, I had no clue of that at the time.

After having my first child, we decided it was important to raise him back home near our families. So, we made the move while I was on maternity leave, and I began teaching that September for a new local school district.

My new school was diverse. There were families living in government subsidized housing, apartment buildings, single family homes, and multiple families under one roof. There were single parent families, multigenerational families, foster families, and older children having guardianship of their younger siblings. There were students born in Canada, Iraq, India, Pakistan, and Serbia. At first, I found it overwhelming to try and understand each of my students' backgrounds, family make-ups, and lived experiences.

When I began teaching at this school, I was fortunate enough to have the same grade as my previous school. Coming off maternity leave, I was thrilled to be teaching the same grade as I learned to balance being a teacher with being a mom. I already had resources, curriculum units, assessment tools, report card comments, and so forth created and ready to go as a foundation. This was going to make transitioning back to teaching as a new mother so much easier . . . or so I thought.

From the first day, I loved my new school. The students were fabulous and the staff was amazing, yet there was one noticeable difference. I wasn't getting any parent phone calls or messages, and there were never parents or caregivers waiting for me before or after school for a quick chat.

I also noticed that when homework was sent home, maybe one-third of my class would bring it back completed, with the rest of my students' saying things like:

"I was at my dad's last night and did my homework, but I forgot my backpack there. I can't get it till I see him again on Saturday."

"I didn't understand the homework and my parents couldn't help me because they don't speak English."

"The police were at my house last night and so . . ."

"I didn't have a pencil at home."

"We have no food at home, and I couldn't concentrate because I was too hungry."

My heart broke. Was I really going to track who did their homework every day when some of my students weren't even having their basic needs met?

That was a huge reality check for me. I realized that, although I was teaching the same grade as at my previous school, nothing was going to be the same.

Every Child Has a Story

My most important message for new teachers is this: every child has a story. If nothing else, remember that every child is unique, has unique circumstances, unique life experiences, a unique home life, a unique brain, and that there are many things that you don't know about each student in your class.

So be curious. Be curious about each of your students. Take the time to connect, listen, ask questions, and get to know their personal story. I promise you that when you know more about your students personally, you will show up for them differently. And that will be crucial for the life trajectory of some of the students you teach.

All Behavior Is a Form of Communication

As a new teacher, you will most likely take student behavior at face value and think that the student who shouts out is trying to be disruptive, the student who doesn't do their schoolwork is being lazy, and the student who can't find his paper is disorganized. Although there will be times where this might be the case, often it is a sign of something more.

When you see undesirable student behavior, I challenge you to stop and ask yourself, *"What is this behavior communicating?"* As a new teacher you may not have all the answers, but with experience, you will learn the typical underlying causes of certain behaviors and begin to develop strategies for supporting these students. As a result, you will be able to minimize these undesirable behaviors that might negatively impact student learning.

In the following chart I highlight some of the most common behaviors teachers observe and offer possible "explanations" for the behavior. It is important to note that these are just sample generalizations and may or may not apply to your students. This list is also not exhaustive in nature.

Behavior	Possible Explanation
Constantly talking or moving around the classroom	• Inability to focus & attend (ADHD) • Anxiety • Nervous system requires a high level of movement
Forgets the directions or what you just told them	• Executive functioning deficits in working memory and/or sustained attention
Takes longer than other students to complete all tasks	• Slow processing speed • Executive functioning deficit in working memory, time management, task initiation and/or sustained attention
Cannot find their pencil, notebook etc. when needed	• Executive functioning deficit in organization

Shouts out constantly but is immediately remorseful	• Executive functioning deficit in impulse control
Shuts down and refuses to re-engage in an activity or schoolwork	• Executive functioning deficit in task initiation, planning & prioritizing and/or cognitive flexibility • Lacks self-confidence • Lacks the precursor skills needed to be successful • Mental health
Struggles to get started with school tasks	• Executive functioning deficit in task initiation, planning & prioritizing and/or working memory • Slow processing speed • Language barrier (ESL)
Struggles transitioning from one task to another or one environment to another (outdoors to indoors, classroom to library, schoolwork to recess, etc.)	• Lacks adaptive skills • Executive functioning deficit in cognitive flexibility • Autism • Anxiety
Has emotional reactions beyond what would be expected or appropriate given the situation and their age	• Executive functioning deficit in emotional control and/or response inhibition • Lacks self-regulation skills • Trauma • Unable to communicate needs • Mental health

As you can see, often when students struggle in school the underlying root cause may be deficits in executive functioning skills. The good news is that there are research-based strategies that work effectively to support students with deficits in one or more areas of executive functioning. When these strategies are implemented and used consistently, most students will experience significant improvements in behavior and academics.

I would recommend taking some time to learn more about the executive functioning processes and their impact on student learning. The following chart gives you a brief description of each:

11 Executive Functioning Skills

Response Inhibition
The ability to stop and think before acting.

Working Memory
The ability to hold information in your mind and use it to complete a task.

Emotional Control
The ability to manage emotions to achieve goals, complete tasks, or control and direct behavior.

Sustained Attention
The ability to keep paying attention to a situation or task despite distractibility, fatigue, or boredom.

Task Initiation
The ability to recognize when it is time to get started on something and begin without procrastination.

Planning and Prioritizing
The ability to create steps to reach a goal and to make decisions about what to focus on.

Organization

The ability to create and maintain systems to keep track of information or materials.

Time Management

The ability to estimate how much time one has, how to allocate it, and how to stay within time limits and deadlines.

Goal-Directed Persistence

The ability to have a goal, and follow through to completion of the goal, without being distracted by competing interests.

Cognitive Flexibility

The ability to change strategies or revise plans when conditions change (adaptability).

Beyond executive functioning deficits or identifiable diagnoses such as Autism, ADHD, and learning disabilities, there are other circumstances that may negatively impact student behavior and learning. This is when knowing your students and connecting with them is pivotal.

Students may be experiencing trauma, mental or physical health issues, parental separation, grief, or instability in their lives. When issues such as these arise, as teachers we often get no "heads up"–which means no official diagnosis or communication from parents. These students show up in our class like they would any other day and we have no idea something is amiss until they either tell us or show us through their behavior.

In my experience students will most often show us rather than tell us.

Once they show you, that is your cue to connect further. When you take the time to connect, listen, and be a safe space for them, you will learn so much about what they are going through and what they need. And sometimes it will break your heart to hear their story.

I can promise you one thing, you will not look at their behavior the same. You will approach it from a place of compassion and understanding. You will go to great lengths to give them what they need. You will be the teacher they remember long after they've finished school, because they knew for certain that you cared about them.

What Is Teacher-Student Connection and Why Does It Matter?

Being connected to your students means knowing the little things about them: what sport they play outside of school, if they have pets, what books they like to read, what they did on the weekend, what games they play at recess, or anything else that is somewhat unique to them.

It also means knowing their personality well enough to know when something is amiss. It means creating a trusting relationship with them. It means making sure they know you care about them personally, regardless of their academic performance.

When you take the time to develop a genuine connection with students, they will go to great lengths to meet your expectations both academically and behaviorally. Why? Because they value their relationship with you, and they know you care.

> Most students come to school to learn and socialize, but there will always be students who come to school to be loved.

Alternatively, when that connection with students is lacking, you will often hear students say things like, *"She doesn't care about me, why should I care about her rules?"*. In general, students don't learn well from teachers they don't like (or rather, teachers they have no connection with).

Most students come to school to learn and socialize, but there will always be students who come to school to be loved.

> **REMINDER**
>
> When developing teacher-student relationships with high school students, it is important to ensure you set firm boundaries to avoid any cross-over between professional and personal.

Connection Before Learning

As teachers, it is our job to set the bar high and help our students reach their fullest potential. The best strategy for doing that is by using your personal connection with students to encourage, support, and celebrate their learning. For some students, you will need to wholeheartedly believe in them before they will believe in themselves.

By developing and continuing to grow your connection with students, you can rest assured that you will get their best from them every day.

Another great way to engage students in the learning process is by allowing them to see your love of learning. Whether you geek out about math, have a love of music, play sports, or are a history buff, when you allow students to witness your excitement, commitment to learning, and your own learning process, it will excite them. Excitement for learning is contagious.

I have a genuine love of "funky socks" (or at least that's what I call them). I've always worn fun socks with assorted colors, patterns, characters . . . you name it. It's just a little thing I enjoy that puts a pep in my step.

I was teaching grade five when my students first took notice. It began with them commenting on my socks, and that quickly spread to a few of the girls randomly wearing fun socks. It then grew to be our tradition to wear funky socks every Friday (to which even the grade five boys joined in). As the weeks went on, I started getting comments from parents about their children being obsessed with funky socks. Apparently, they were constantly begging them to get new ones. When that didn't work, they started mismatching their socks to make their own (which was driving their parents crazy).

It was amazing how our entire class connected over something as random as socks. I was able to leverage that connection to build classroom community and develop a sense of belonging, which in turn strengthened my relationship with my students. Then, of course, I could further leverage that connection to get the best from each of them as learners.

So, give it some thought. Do you have a personal interest that you could connect with your students about? If so, I would encourage you to share your interests with them as appropriate.

Connection Before Redirection or Compliance

I cannot overstate the importance of connecting with students *before* expecting compliance. This is especially true for older students. If you have zero connection with a student and you think that you are going to come along and tell them to take their hat off in the hallway or go back to class, you are probably mistaken. Unless they fear you, but I digress.

To expect compliance on school rules, classroom expectations, or anything else for that matter, you must first have a connection with the student. This is even more imperative for older students and students that exhibit challenging behaviors. In their world, they need to have a *reason* to listen to you. I can tell you for certain, **because you are the teacher** is not going to be one of them.

Putting in the time to establish connections with students goes well beyond your own classroom. Take the time to say good morning to students in the hallway, hold a door for them, or pay them a genuine compliment. These are small ways to begin to build these connections with other students in the school beyond just your own class. By doing this, you will be in a better position to expect compliance from them in the future should the need arise.

I would also encourage you to learn the names of students that might come to you in future years by interacting with them whenever possible. It is never too early to begin building those student relationships.

I have witnessed teachers over the years go head-to-head with students because they would not comply with a request the teacher was making. Typically, the standoff continues for some time and eventually escalates into something even bigger than the original issue.

When this happens, it's typically because the teacher and student do not have a connection. Often, the student has never been in their class or had any meaningful interaction with the teacher. Regardless, the situation could most likely be avoided if a human connection was established first, before making the request.

I remember walking up to such a situation where a staff member was demanding that a student go into her classroom because the break was over, and she was the only one left in the hallway.

The student refused and sat slumped on the floor with her arms crossed. The staff member became frustrated, and stated to me as I walked up, "She just won't listen," throwing her hands in the air and walking away.

I squatted down beside her and asked if she was upset? She nodded her head in agreement. I asked her what she needed to feel better? She told me she needed time by herself for a few minutes. So, I asked, "If I let you sit here by yourself for a few minutes, do you think you will be ready to go into class?" She agreed she would.

I then let her teacher know that I was in the hallway with her and asked if it was okay if she came in in a few minutes? Her classroom teacher was fine with that. I gave her some space by standing further down the hallway while she sat there (I assume to regulate her emotions).

> This student knew what she needed; she also needed an adult who would hear her.

After a few minutes, she came over to me and said she was ready to go to class.

This student knew what she needed; she also needed an adult who would hear her. By taking a moment to connect with her and find out what she needed, there was no standoff. There was no compliance issue. Just a child trying to do what she needed to do to be okay.

"You didn't have a class full of other students and had time to stand in the hallway and watch her!"

Granted, I wasn't busy with a classroom full of children and was able to give her what she needed, but the point remains. With a little creative thinking, there is typically a way to meet a student's needs or, at the very least, find a compromise that works for both of you.

She could have sat alone in the corner of the classroom, or she could have sat at her desk and been allowed to put her head down. She could have also been given permission to go to another area in the school with support staff or an administrator and have the time and space she needed.

Unless and until a child's basic needs are met, learning is not going to happen.

5 Steps for Redirecting Students

1. Approach them at their eye level.
2. Make a personal connection before addressing the behavior or expectation.
3. Once a human connection has been established, explain what you need from them **and why.**
4. Allow them to respond.
5. Request compliance.

I would be remiss if I didn't note that some children have complex profiles. Children with complex profiles often have a behavior plan (or something of that nature) in place. For these children, it is important to know what steps the behavior plan outlines and follow them accordingly. If you are unsure of the steps, it would be best to ask for someone else to support the student who has that knowledge and experience.

Connection Before Discipline

Another pivotal time for student connection is when discipline is involved. When a student has engaged in a behavior where there needs to be consequences, it is important that we differentiate the behavior from the child. Meaning, it needs to be crystal clear to the student that while the behavior is unacceptable, we still like and value them as a person. In addition, we need to commit to giving students a clean slate once discipline has been served.

Students are still children. We cannot hold them to the same standards that we expect from adults when their executive functioning skills are not fully developed. We must account for the fact that our students do not have fully developed brains and continue to work to support their development, which in turn, will minimize these behaviors or "poor choices".

To do that, we must have a strong teacher-student connection as the foundation. Knowing they've disappointed a teacher they value might be the most impactful consequence a student can receive. To risk losing that connection, (or your belief in them) will outdo any consequence a school can give.

What Did You Need as a Child?

Another way to look at this is to think back to what you needed as a student. What did you need that you may or may not have received? What would have made a difference for you?

Also consider your own favorite teachers. Why were they your favorite? What did they do that was different from other teachers? I can guarantee it wasn't about their lesson plans. It was about the way they made you feel. The connection that you had with them. The way you *knew* they cared about you.

The Opportunity to Make a Difference

How fortunate are we as teachers to do a job that impacts the lives of children? We have this opportunity daily to show up for kids, make a difference, and to be the person they need that day. Many adults can remember the moment that a teacher changed the trajectory of their life. How amazing is it to have that opportunity, simply by being a teacher?

> Never underestimate the difference you can make in a child's life.

Never underestimate the difference you can make in a child's life. And know that often, it is for the child that you would least expect. I've had students come up to me years later and tell me that I was their favorite teacher, or remind me of something we did, or a book we read, and I had no idea it impacted them the way it did.

Show up to your classroom every day and embrace the magnitude of the gift you've been given by becoming a teacher. Yes, there will be long, challenging days. But at the end of your career, it will be the relationship that you built with students that you will remember and value most.

Final Thoughts

Many teachers get caught up in all the must-dos of the job (lesson planning, assessment, marking, writing report cards, etc.). At times, you may find that you are on autopilot just trying to keep all the proverbial balls in the air. And with an enormous curriculum to cover, it can become like a checklist of things to just get through.

> Remember that you teach children, not curriculum.

But as a new teacher, I challenge you to always remember this: remember that you teach children, not curriculum.

ACTION STEPS

The following are some suggestions for building genuine connections with your students:

Allow your students to get to know you.

- Tell them stories about your pets.
- Update them regularly on how your favorite sports team is doing.
- Share stories about your hobby or passion.
- Where funky socks or silly ties.

The goal is to help them get to know things about you that make you human, and not just their teacher.

Start each day off right.

- Always be ready to greet students at the door
- Say good morning, use their name, and comment on something positive about them.
- Use this time to take each student's "temperature" and look for those students who may not be "school ready." Then determine what you need to do to help that student turn their morning around.

Make it a point throughout the day to connect personally with each student.

- Let them tell you a story they want to share, a joke, show you their drawing, and so on.
- If you know of something happening in their non-school life, ask about it, such as their new pet, their game last night, their sleepover at Grandma's house, or any other nugget of information you can connect on.

Know when to prioritize mental health and self-esteem over academic tasks.

- If a student is not "school ready," no learning will happen until they are, so always prioritize their personal needs over academics. By doing so, you are once again communicating that you care.

End each day by giving students a reason to be excited about coming to school the next day.

- Give them a sneak peek of what you have in

store for tomorrow at school, such as a new game, a fun science experiment, an enjoyable book, or anything that will give them something to look forward to.

- Tell them about something you're doing after school that day and let them know you'll give them an update tomorrow, such as taking your pet to the vet, getting a haircut, wearing your new socks, taking your child to the dentist, or anything else that is appropriate to share with them.

LESSON #4: Parents Are Essential to Student Success

Stress-Free Parent Communication and Involvement

Author's Note: The term "parent" is used in this chapter for simplicity and is intended to include guardians or family members that assume a parental role for students.

Parent involvement in a child's education is imperative to a student's success socially, emotionally, and academically at school. As a new teacher, it is important to embrace a parent's role in their child's education. Fostering relationships with the parents of your students through open communication will make your job both easier and more enjoyable.

New teachers are often anxious about conversations with parents. They worry that they might not know exactly how to answer a parent's questions or address concerns. I've even seen some new teachers worry that they might cry if the parent gets upset or angry. My advice to new teachers is to approach these conversations head on, without delay, and to communicate with genuine care and concern for their child.

Most parents can accept that a teacher may not have all the answers or know exactly how to navigate a situation when they believe that the teacher genuinely likes, cares for, and wants the best for their child.

Parents are not people to be feared but rather embraced as allies. Building positive relationships with the parents of your students early in the school year will set you at ease. It will also give you confidence when the time comes to engage in conversations about their child's learning.

Establishing Communication Early in the School Year

The importance of making calls home during the first two weeks of the school year cannot be overstated. Making time for these calls will go a long way with parents in setting the tone for all future conversations about their child. They don't need to be lengthy, rather just a few minutes to say hello, introduce yourself, tell them how much you enjoy having their child in your class, and then end with something positive about their child. That's it.

Parents will appreciate that you made that effort, and it will put them at ease that you've established positive communication with them early on.

You could also take the time to let them know the best ways to get in touch with you, or even ask if there is anything they'd like to share with you about their child.

The key is to keep it brief, but genuine, as you have many calls to make. I would suggest setting a goal to call three parents each school day until you've gotten through your entire class. That said, you may also wish to prioritize which parents to call first if you feel that would be beneficial.

When you first get started making those calls, having a checklist in front of you of the things you want to communicate might be advantageous. After you've made a few calls, you'll settle into a "script" and won't really need the checklist any further.

First Phone Call Checklist

- ✓ Introduce myself
- ✓ Positive comment about their child
- ✓ How best to communicate with me
- ✓ Anything they'd like me to know about their child

You can also use this first phone call as an opportunity to start your documentation for each student by making some brief notes after each call regarding who you talked to, on what date, and anything discussed that you feel is important to note.

How and where you record documentation is an individual decision. However, setting good habits early and making it easy for yourself will help to ensure you stay consistent and have everything in one secure place.

REMINDER

Refrain from calling from your personal cell phone and giving parents access to your phone number. Always call from a school phone. If you must call from your cell phone, ensure the number will not be visible.

Communicate Often

An informed parent is generally a happy parent.

Parents love to know what is happening at school with their children. An informed parent is generally a happy parent.

There are endless ways for you to communicate with parents throughout the school year. A class newsletter, email, your school platform, or phone calls are all excellent ways for reaching parents. The key is to choose the avenues that work best for you and then remain consistent so that parents get into a routine and know what to expect.

For example, you could send home a newsletter or calendar at the beginning of each month and then one class-wide message to parents each Friday sharing highlights from the week (you might even include pictures).

REMINDER

Familiarize yourself with your school board's policy on student photos and adhere to their guidelines, as well as any additional parent preferences for individual students, when sharing photos.

A classroom newsletter or calendar will keep your students and parents organized and let them know what's coming up so they can be prepared. A quick message at the end of each week allows parents a glimpse into their child's learning and school life so that they feel connected and have some starting points for conversations with their children about school.

A Sample Friday Message

> Hey parents!
>
> Your children had a fantastic week of learning!
>
> This week we began reading the novel **The One and Only Ivan**, and they are hooked! They've amazed me with their insights and questions. Ask them about Ivan!
>
> They are also very excited that we've finally come to the end of our science unit and it's time to build their structures! Here's a sneak peek of what they've been working on so far. We are still in need of recycling materials so feel free to send more in on Monday.
>
> Enjoy your weekend,
>
> Ms. Hazel

REMINDER

Representation matters. Do your best to ensure that all parents can see their children in the messages and pictures that you share. Parents will notice and wonder why there are never pictures of their child.

Which Format Is Best?

For general communication with parents, there isn't necessarily a "right" answer to which format is best, as each family's situation is unique. At times, parents may let you know that they prefer phone calls, emails, or in person meetings. Make note of these preferences and do your best to accommodate them. Often, these requests stem from parent limitations such as working hours, custody agreements, access to technology, and other factors.

However, I would strongly encourage you to stay away from using social media platforms with your class or to communicate with parents. Most school boards have a preferred platform that is available to staff, students, and parents. Your best bet is to get in the habit of making this platform work for you.

"I can't stop the parents from contacting me on social media."

While you can't stop parents from messaging you on social media, you don't need to respond to them on a social media platform. Simply move the conversation to your school district's approved platform and ask them to direct any messages to you there. Most parents will respect that and refrain from doing it again. You can also consider using a variation of your name for your social media profiles, making it a bit harder to be found.

REMINDER

Never post any messages about or pictures of your students on social media. Most school districts and professional teachers' organizations have strict policies and procedures for the use of social media. Make sure that you adhere to them.

The question of which format is best will typically come into play when communicating with individual parents. Unfortunately, as an educator you will have situations where you need to be very cognizant of which communication methods you choose to use with certain parents during your career.

This is typically a result of some sort of breakdown in communication with a parent. When this happens, you need to carefully consider whether your future communications need to be written, verbal, or even only face-to-face with someone else present.

The benefit of using written communication is that you can keep a copy for your records of exactly what and when you communicated. The pitfall is that parents are then at liberty to share what you've written with others, often on social media.

The benefit of verbal communication is that you are in a better position to ensure that the message you intend to communicate is the message received by the parent. It also allows for a human connection where hopefully the parent can feel your genuine care and concern for their child. However, the pitfall here is that a parent may take what you've said and twist it to fit their narrative, which then becomes he said, she said.

My best advice for teachers when communication with a parent begins to break down is to have all further communication be face-to-face, with a colleague present. Ideally it would be your administrator. However, you could also bring in another teacher that works with the child, such as a rotary teacher or special education teacher.

Navigating Difficult Conversations

There will be times in your teaching career where you will need to have conversations with parents that are difficult to navigate. Perhaps they are of a sensitive nature, or you need to communicate information to a parent that you're not sure they are ready to hear.

These conversations are tough. They will get easier as you gain more experience, but initially you might feel anxious. My advice would be to enlist the support of a more experienced colleague or even one who may know the family well, such as the child's previous teacher or a sibling's teacher. Ask your colleague to walk through the conversation you need to have with you, focusing on a positive tone for the delivery of the message and carefully selecting the words you will use.

It is best to be straightforward with parents and give them a direct message yet be kind and gentle in the delivery. The goal is to leave them feeling optimistic about their child's future. And remember to smile–parents can sense if you're feeling anxious, and that will, in turn, make them anxious.

Conversations around *potential* learning disabilities, indicators of autism, ADHD, bullying, gender identity, high school pathways, and so forth are difficult but sometimes necessary for you to have with parents. Most times you will find that parents already have concerns in their own minds but haven't been ready to verbalize them.

Remind parents that many children have excelled under the same circumstances and be ready with a plan of support. This will give them the sense of hope they need during this moment.

Never share your concerns with parents without having a plan for support ready. Parents will always want to know what the plan is to help their child. You need to be prepared to answer that question, even if you need to look to your colleagues for help in determining those supports.

As a learning support teacher, I would often sit in on meetings when homeroom teachers needed to have difficult conversations with parents. I have been the parent on the receiving end of difficult conversations about my own children and have learned first-hand how important it is to choose your words carefully and deliver the message with compassion and optimism.

Carefully selecting the words used to communicate is another skill that will develop with practice. In the beginning,

I would suggest spending time before meetings to determine exactly what you want to say and consider the words you will use to share the information. Here are some examples:

Instead of . . .	Try this . . .
I think your child has ADHD.	Kai seems to struggle to attend and focus during lessons.
Your child often yells and screams during class.	Nasir struggles to regulate his emotions at school. Do you see this at home?
Your child has many incomplete assignments and is falling behind in class.	Morgan's brain needs more time to process information than her peers, so it takes her longer to complete tasks.
He is disorganized and can never find his things.	Leo would benefit from having an organization system at school where everything is color-coded and labeled.
I think your child has autism.	Have you noticed that Talia (insert behaviors you are seeing)? Is this the same at home? I would recommend sharing this information with your doctor.
Your child isn't learning to read.	Blair is not currently at the benchmark level in reading.
Your child is mean to the other kids.	Mateo struggles to make positive connections with his peers.

Teachers are not medical professionals. After many years of teaching, you may come to recognize indicators which suggest that a certain diagnosis may be appropriate. However, teachers are not qualified to make a diagnosis and should refrain from such statements.

It is also important to know when to involve your administrator, which we will discuss a bit further into the chapter.

No Parent Likes Surprises

> No parent should be caught off guard by the grades or comments on their child's report card.

Another crucial time for communicating with parents is ahead of report cards. The rule of thumb here is that no parent should be surprised. No parent should be caught off guard by the grades or comments on their child's report card. If you are in regular contact with parents, there should never be any surprises.

Rather than wait for the report card to go home and the parent to schedule an interview with you, call ahead and have a conversation with them about their child's current learning progress. Let them know what to expect. And, again, have a plan ready to share that will support their child's learning struggles.

If a parent still chooses to schedule an interview, have evidence of their child's learning progress ready to discuss; show them samples from their child's schoolwork and assessment data. Also, give them suggestions for how to support their child's development at home.

As a parent, watching your child struggle is heartbreaking. Having concrete ways to help move your child forward allows a parent to be proactive and gives them a way to be involved in supporting their child.

Not All Parent Communication Needs a Response

An important aspect of developing your parent communication skills is knowing when a message from a parent does not need a response.

You might get messages from parents who are frustrated and need to vent, who are looking to engage you in a non-productive back and forth, or that attack you personally. These types of messages are better answered with silence. I would suggest signing your initials to indicate that you've received the message, but not to respond any further. If the message is a voicemail, write a brief note acknowledging that it has been received.

Messages like these are typically sent under duress when a parent is emotionally elevated. I have found that most parents will regret sending it and wish that they could take it back. By not engaging, you are allowing them to retreat without further incident.

However, you will experience parents that are going to double down on their message and demand a response. These situations are best handled with a face-to-face meeting while having a colleague or administrator present. Again, I would not suggest responding directly to what was said, but rather by asking when they are able to come in and meet with you to discuss further.

The 24-Hour Rule

On the other hand, there will be times that you are emotionally charged and feel like firing off a message to a parent. This is where the 24-hour rule comes into play.

Never send a message when you are feeling emotionally elevated. You will not only regret it, but it may also end up being shared with others (on social media, in the local newspaper, with the superintendent's office), and might even put you in a position to be disciplined or even terminated.

Instead, give it twenty-four hours. If after twenty-four hours you still feel that you need to send the message, at least you will (hopefully) be in a calmer state and thinking more rationally. I would also suggest having a colleague you trust read over the message before you hit send.

Asking Questions and Listening to Understand

Another key component to parent communication is developing your active listening skills. When you can be fully present in the moment with parents, and not only hear but understand what they are saying and where it is coming from, parents will notice and be more willing to share.

When we genuinely listen to what parents are saying, without feeling the need to immediately respond, we learn things that help us make informed decisions as educators and as compassionate human beings.

Knowing when to ask a question, and what question to ask, will serve you well with both students and parents. When parents feel that they are genuinely listened to and heard, it builds a trusting, productive partnership.

I remember having several meetings as a school team with a mom regarding her son's mental health. We were seeing negative behaviors at school, and he was communicating things to his peers and teachers that had us very concerned for his mental state.

The principal, homeroom teacher, and I (as the learning support teacher) had spoken with mom at length about our concerns. We gave her contact information for community services that could help, suggesting also that she make an appointment with their family doctor.

A few weeks passed and Mom still had not contacted any agencies to inquire about services for her son. She was even reluctant to make him a doctor's appointment. She was adamant that she was helping him at home and that he was going to be fine.

We gently asked her why she was hesitating to get her son help? She broke down in tears and shared that as a child she was apprehended from her mother and put into foster care; her mom was deemed unfit to be a parent. The trauma of that experience made her promise to herself she would never let that happen to her child.

In her mind, she thought that her son's struggles with mental health were a direct result of her parenting, and that if she were to seek services for him, it would automatically lead to her son being taken away and put into foster care. That was the story she was telling herself that kept her from getting him help.

Through our ongoing conversations, our team had built a strong partnership with this parent, and she trusted us as professionals. We were able to understand and validate her emotions, yet still encourage her to seek support. Because she trusted us, she moved forward with reaching out for help despite her personal fears, and both her and her son are in a much better place as a result.

As your journey through your career continues, you will learn that often, the parents of your students have had similar school experiences as their child. Children with a learning disability might have a parent with a learning disability, children that are being bullied might have a parent who was bullied, and so forth.

Therefore, when parents show up to these conversations, they bring with them all the emotions of their own childhood experiences. When parents refuse to engage with the school, it might be because of the trauma around their own school experiences as a child and could have nothing to do with you as the teacher or not wanting to help their child.

Sometimes, we need to give parents grace and the space to get to a place where we can have these conversations with them. Genuinely seeking to understand and asking the right questions is a gateway to building that relationship.

Following are some examples of questions you could ask parents to begin to develop that relationship:

- How does Nisha feel about school?
- What would you like to see Calvin improve at?
- Why do you think Kamari does that?
- How can I help Simone?
- What works for Adair at home?
- What else would you like me to know?
- Do you have any suggestions?
- Do you know what Mila's triggers are?
- What does Harmony like to do outside of school?

Asking questions and genuinely listening to the answers is the foundation for building great partnerships with parents.

When to Loop in Your Administrator

Many new teachers feel uncertain when trying to decide if they need to talk to their administrator about something happening in their classroom or with the parents of their students. Typically, new teachers fall into one of two categories: they overshare and tell their administrators everything (meaning telling them too much; more than they need to know) or they tell them nothing because they are nervous about approaching them. Neither is a good scenario.

It is important to find that sweet spot and know when you need to loop them in, and when it is something that you can navigate yourself. If you're unsure, asking a trusted colleague their opinion is always a good idea.

> **REMINDER**
>
> Remember not to use specifics when discussing student or parent situations with colleagues. Rather, just share the nature of the situation without using names or identifying factors

You'll want to talk to your administrator if the following scenarios arise:

- It involves the safety of staff, students, or parents.
- If you expect that a parent is going to contact your administrator, superintendent, or trustees about the situation.
- If you feel that a parent may take to social media or traditional media with their opinions or complaints.
- If an accusation is being made against you (directly or indirectly).
- If a parent indicates that they are contacting their lawyer.
- If you need to make a call to child services.

As a new teacher, if you're unsure, I would err on the side of speaking to your administrator. With more experience, you will learn better when to loop them in and when to handle things yourself.

On the flip side, if you are prone to handling everything yourself and struggle to communicate with your administrator, you're going to need to develop some strategies. There will be times when it is a must, and you need to be able to do it.

If it feels easier, you could always email to let them know you need to connect about a situation and then wait for them to come to you. This is a good option when time is not of the essence, as they may not get to you right away.

> **REMINDER**
> It is crucial to document all conversations, messages, or meetings with the parents of your students. It is impossible to predict when you might be called to share your documentation or why. But inevitably, it will happen at some point in your career. It's best to always be prepared.

Home-School Partnerships

The relationships you develop with parents during your teaching career will typically be positive, and most importantly, beneficial to your students' success. Parental involvement in a child's education is a high predictor of social, emotional, and academic success at school. It is essential that parents have an opportunity to be involved.

A great strategy for encouraging a home-school partnership is to cultivate opportunities for parents to be involved in their child's learning. There are many ways to do that.

"It's just one more thing that I don't have time for."

The good news is that you are in full control of the opportunities you provide to parents. Once you've determined when and how you would like to involve parents, set up structures or a system that is easy to implement and maintain. You could start with just one or two opportunities at first, and then expand the opportunities in future years.

Again, this may be a bit daunting at first, but I promise you it will pay dividends for you as the teacher and have significant benefits for your students.

> ## REMINDER
>
> "Parents" look different for each family. When extending opportunities, remember to use inclusive language and be open to more than just *parent* participation. For some students, it may be an older sibling, grandparent, or family friend that attends school events. When family members are unable to attend, you could also consider inviting a sibling that attends the same school.

Let's have a look at a few ways you could involve parents in your classroom.

Volunteering

There are a variety of ways for parents to volunteer in your classroom that don't require too much preparation on your part and can make less work for you. Art lessons, science experiments, practicing for a school concert or play (or any other activities that are busy and require you to try to be in many places at the same time) are great opportunities to involve parents.

You can put students into groups and have parents provide support to a specific group, or alternatively, just float around and help where needed. It is also fantastic to have parents available to set up or clean up; again, making less work for you.

Field Trips

Most field trips require a certain student-to-adult ratio. However, there is no harm in bringing extra parents also should it be feasible. Students typically love to have their parents along for the experience. It also makes things easier for you to have more eyes on your students, ensuring everyone is safe and accounted for.

Special Occasions

I use the term "special occasions" loosely, to define any time that family members can be invited to watch or participate in student-led activities or attend an event. Beyond the traditional holidays, you could also invite parents in to read with their child, play math games, attend a poetry café or science fair, watch drama presentations, visit the book fair, and so forth.

Parent-Led Presentations

This is one of my favorites. My second year teaching I had the idea to invite parents in to talk to my class about their career. They were also invited to bring in any "tools of the trade," as appropriate, to show students what they were and demonstrate how they were used.

We had our "career day" the last period of the day every other Friday. The students absolutely loved it! They loved learning about real world things, getting to try different tools, and watching their parents talk to their classmates. My students had the opportunity to see a respirator and learn how it works, try on pieces of firefighting equipment, learn what it is like to fly a plane and ask questions of a commercial pilot, and so much more. They were completely engaged and looked forward to these days.

To organize this, I simply sent home a parent note and attached a schedule with all the dates available for presentations. Parents were asked to check which dates they would be available to come in to speak to the class (if interested). From there, I took all the responses and made a master schedule. I then sent home the master schedule, and each parent knew well in advance their date and time.

We also discussed as a class how to make proper introductions and how to properly thank a guest speaker. Each child was responsible for introducing and thanking their parent before and after their presentation, respectively. The parents seemed to really enjoy this, and the kids felt proud to recognize their parents. Students whose parents were unable to present partnered with a friend to introduce and thank their parent.

This is just one way to create opportunities for parent-led presentations in your classroom. Depending on your school community, it may look different. I would encourage you to consider the strengths of your community, the availability of your families, and any barriers to participation that may arise. Ideally, you'd like to provide an opportunity that would make sense for most, if not all, of your community of parents.

In this community, "career day" worked nicely.

At-Home Learning (Not Homework)

Providing at-home learning opportunities is different than homework. These are optional activities that parents can choose to do with their children to extend the learning happening in the classroom.

The range of activities can be vast and varied, but at minimum should be age-appropriate and considerate of your school community. Here is a brief list of suggested activities to give you a starting point:

- Books related to content subjects for parents and children to read together, which can springboard into conversations about the topic.

- Links to websites, learning materials, or online games related to school subjects and curriculum.

- Math- or literacy-based activities or games.

- Suggestions for community events, landmarks, or museums that tie into student learning topics.
- A list of functional skills for students to practice such as telling time, following a recipe, or writing a letter or email.

These at-home learning suggestions could be incorporated into your class newsletter, (or other parent communications) as recommended activities to support their child's current learning at school each month.

Parents often ask how they can support their child at school. Encouraging and providing opportunities for at-home learning is a perfect way for parents to get involved in supporting their child's academic progress. They will also be more informed about what is happening in the classroom and will be able to ask better questions than *"how was school today?"*

Final Thoughts

Strong parent communication skills are imperative for teachers. Developing them early and practicing them often will build your confidence and allow these conversations to eventually become second nature.

If you need to start by making yourself notes before a phone call or asking a colleague to read things over first before you send a message, do it. We all need to start somewhere. Do not overthink it or procrastinate, as that only makes things more daunting.

Like any other skills you've learned, communicating effectively with parents takes practice and will get better with experience. Similarly, welcoming parents into your classroom environment also gets easier and more comfortable with time.

Do your best to view parents as partners in their children's education rather than judge and jury on your abilities as a teacher. Most parents are lovely and just want the best for their children. They are willing to do their part if they understand what their role is and how best to support their child.

When I was a brand-new teacher, the parents of my students "loved" me. Not because I was a curriculum expert or planning stellar lessons, but because their children enjoyed coming to school and came home happy. At the end of the day, that is what is most important to parents–their child's happiness.

I took that win for what it was and, eventually, developed my skills and practice to a level that I felt confident with. But as a beginning teacher, I was thrilled that my students were loving school, and my parents were loving me. The rest came with time.

ACTION STEPS

Here are some suggestions for getting started with developing strong parent partnerships:

- Create a blank classroom newsletter or calendar template that you can reuse each month.

- Keep a copy of your student's contact information at your fingertips for easy access when you need to make a call or send a message.

- Decide where and how you are going to record documentation throughout the school year and set the habit early.

- Clearly communicate to parents the best ways to contact you (i.e., via email, school platform, phone call, before school, etc.) and set clear boundaries on your working hours.

- Make a checklist of what you want to discuss before calling or meeting with a parent.

- Set a goal at the beginning of each school year for "first phone calls" and stick to it.
- Brainstorm ways that you could involve the families of your students in the classroom this school year.
- Locate your school district's policies and procedures on the use of social media and familiarize yourself with it.

LESSON #5: Never Ask Your Principal If They Have a Minute

Fostering a Professional Relationship with Your Administration

As a new teacher, administrators can seem intimidating to interact with. The pace of a school moves quickly, and principals and vice-principals are tasked with many responsibilities. Trying to get a moment of their time can seem impossible, and when you are able to get a meeting, you typically only get a "moment" before they are on to the next thing (especially if it's during the school day).

So, as a teacher it is imperative to understand when and how to communicate effectively with your administrators, as well as how to build a good working relationship.

Laying the Foundation

Building a strong working relationship with your administration team starts from the moment you first meet. Ideally, you want the first meeting to be light and friendly, leaving them with a positive first impression.

Initially, try to avoid asking the million and one questions that are going through your head as a new teacher. Instead, save those questions for your teaching partners and other education colleagues. If no one has told you already, secretaries and custodians are a teacher's best friends.

Beyond the first meeting, when you need to approach your administrator, always remember these two things: they are human and they were once teachers, too.

"I don't even have my class list yet."

"I don't know my schedule."

"I'm missing core resources."

Principals know the questions you have, how you're feeling, and what you need and want to know. They will do their best to get you everything needed to be successful as soon as they can. They also have many school-wide roles and responsibilities that you don't see. Just like you, they are being pulled in many directions with a seemingly never-ending "to-do" list.

> Veteran teachers know that it is best to write everything in pencil, not pen, at the beginning of a new school year.

In addition, each new year starts with instability as schools receive new registrations, current students move, staffing assignments change, and so forth. Veteran teachers know that it is best to write everything in pencil, not pen, at the beginning of a new school year.

Building a strong working relationship also takes time. Administrators have a large staff of teachers, support staff, and other education workers as well as a school full of students and parents who all need their time and attention. They are simultaneously trying to establish relationships with everyone else who is also new to the building in any capacity.

Be patient, allow them some grace, and respect their time. Allow them to get to know you personally as well as professionally and take the time to get to know them. Ask how their day is going or if there is anything they need. The best way to find joy in your career as a teacher is to cultivate your relationships with staff, students, and parents by connecting on a personal level, and that includes your administrators.

The Role of Administrators

Administrators are an extension of the school district and, as such, are often tasked with implementing the school boards and government's mandates at the school level. They must manage everything in a school from health and safety to being the instructional leader to fielding complaints from neighbors, and everything in between.

They also have their own set of people they must answer to, such as superintendents, parents, students, trustees, the community, parent council, and the various unions.

Their job is to look at things from a whole school perspective; to make decisions that benefit the school community as a whole and most importantly, the students. There will be times when something that is in the best interest of the school community does not align with the preferences of teachers.

What makes sense from our teacher lens might not be what makes sense from the whole school lens or what is best for students. Administrators are tasked with making those tough decisions. Those decisions might not necessarily be the ones they want to make (when considering only their teaching staff), but ones they must make despite the dissension.

Being an administrator can be isolating at times. As teachers, we have an abundance of colleagues in our school who understand and can appreciate our daily experiences and demands. Administrators might have one colleague (and often none) who can understand and appreciate their daily experiences and the demands placed on them.

As much as we need to build positive working relationships with our principals and vice-principals, they too need relationships with us for their own happiness and mental health.

Administrators Are Regular People

Administrators are regular people. They are not trying to *make you* feel insecure as a new teacher or judge you. They too have their own personalities, competencies, strengths, and weaknesses.

Over the course of your career, you will work with administrators who you completely gel with and are similar in personality to you. You will also have others who are completely different from you, and you might find it challenging to relate to them (and that's okay). The goal is always to build a good working relationship, not find a new best friend.

Administrators have personal lives, families, struggles, their own children, and such (much the same as you). They understand that you cannot be at 100 percent every day. They can relate to the fact that you will have off days, be ill, have family emergencies, and so forth.

If you find yourself needing an extra day to complete your report cards or IEPs, or that you can't stay after school for a staff meeting, talk to them. Every educator will have times when they are unable to meet a demand, expectation, or timeline. Your administrator will have those times too. They get it. They are human.

That said, an issue may arise if it becomes a habit. If during every reporting period you are asking for an extension to complete your report cards, then your principal could begin to see this as an issue. There is a difference between the occasional occurrence and a constant need. Do not make it a habit. That might lead to a strain on your working relationship with your administrator. Every time you ask for an allowance from them, it causes them to need to adjust their own workload and timelines. And you are only one member of their staff. Imagine what can happen with a staff of forty-plus teachers.

Appeal to their human nature, but don't take advantage of it.

Ask For What You Need

Many times, I've witnessed teachers with valid needs (that usually can be met) afraid to approach their administrator for resources or assistance. I've seen teachers make do with a half class set of textbooks when more were available, miss out on important family milestones when adjustments could have been made to allow for them to attend, and suffer in silence when help was available.

If there is something you need, either personally or professionally, I encourage you to ask. The answer will always be "no" if you never ask. Typically, if you come with suggestions for a solution or a way to navigate a situation, then it is easy for your principal to say yes. Make it easy for them.

In terms of resources, school budgets are tight. However, if there is a need for either one or all your students, ask. You're really asking for your students, not for yourself. You are advocating to better meet their needs. And as previously stated, come prepared with the specifics: what do you need, how many, and what is the cost? Have a link ready to send them for an order if you are asking for a physical resource.

As a learning support teacher, I often advocated for the needs of individual students. I would borrow things that I thought might support a student's learning or behavior needs such as bouncy bands, wobble stools, laptops or tablets, sensory tools, and access to software.

Once we knew that the tool was having a positive impact for the student, I could then take that data to my principal and share those findings to advocate for the student's need. When presented with the data, it is hard to say no to meeting the needs of students. Administrators can usually get creative and find funds when necessary.

Involving Them in Your Classroom

A great strategy for building a relationship with your administrators is to invite them into your classroom to highlight your students' learning and the positive things going on in your class.

> Most administrators enjoy being involved in the learning process and will welcome an opportunity to put down their "must-dos" for a moment to engage with kids.

Most administrators enjoy being involved in the learning process and will welcome an opportunity to put down their "must-dos" for a moment to engage with kids. As human beings, they need these connections with kids to persevere through the difficult aspects of their job. It also reminds them of the reason they got into education and what all their hard work is for.

These are some ideal times to send out that invitation:

- At the end of a unit when students are consolidating their learning
- During an activity that students are really excited about

- When your students want to show off a new skill

- When you invite parents into the classroom for a special day with their children

- When older students help or mentor younger students

- When your students do something for others, such as the school community or neighborhood

Essentially, any time you want to celebrate your students and the great things happening in your classroom.

Another strategy, if your administrator is agreeable, is to send students to their office for "good news visits." Good news visits are for times when you are looking to celebrate the accomplishment or effort of an individual student.

Sending students to the office with a *ticket* will help your principal better understand what is being celebrated so that they can engage the students in a meaningful conversation. This is especially helpful for students who are shy or not sure how to communicate why they are there.

A good news ticket can be as simple as a strip of paper in the following example.

Good News Ticket!

Student Name: __________________

Reason for Visit: _______________

You could send students for good news visits when:

- They master a new skill or concept

- They make improvements in an area of learning
- They were kind, generous, or helpful
- They need a boost to their self-confidence

Really, these visits are helpful for any reason that a student would benefit from being celebrated and to encourage future behavior or efforts.

I would recommend connecting with your administrators before sending anyone down for a good news visit. There may need to be parameters around what days and times are best for such visits, as school offices can be hectic and busy.

Alternatively, you could send a quick email letting them know that you have students who would like to have a good news visit, and then let your administrator call them down to their office when it's a good time. You'd like to avoid getting a student all hyped about a good news visit and then find out that they were turned away because the principal was busy.

When you take it upon yourself to give your administrators opportunities to engage with you and your students, it not only serves to strengthen your relationship and build their confidence in you as an educator, but also allows you to become more comfortable interacting with them.

And let's face it, they are going to come into your classroom whether you like to or not. It might as well be when you are expecting it and have great things going on for them to witness.

Consult Your Colleagues Often

As a new teacher, it may take you some time to learn the ropes in terms of communicating with your administration. You may feel awkward about when to talk to them or how to approach them. That's normal. Eventually you will get the hang of it, and it will become easier.

Until then, look to your colleagues' examples and run things by them first if you're unsure. Many times, what you think is a question for your administrator can be answered by someone else. Many schools also have their own culture about how things work. Asking your colleagues could save you from engaging them unnecessarily.

I remember during my first two weeks as a new teacher feeling very confused as I listened to other teachers talking in the staffroom. They would discuss dates, events, and information that were all news to me. I spent days wondering how they all knew these things. Were there memos I was missing? How did they all know these things?

I was thinking of going to speak to my principal but was nervous about approaching him. So, I finally got up the courage to ask another teacher. Turns out, I had a board email! I had no idea. At no point leading up to my first school year did anyone tell me that we had a board email address (please keep in mind that this was 1998).

Thankfully, she took the time to show me where to find it and how to access it with my credentials. And, voila! There was all the information I had been missing. I was so happy that I decided to check with my colleague first.

Ideally, you only want to engage your administrator when it is something that must go through them or when no one else is in the position to answer your question. Not because they are so important that they don't have time for you, but rather out of respect for their time and the demands of their role.

When and How to Communicate

There are times where it is necessary to address your questions or concerns to your administrator. With endless options for communication, here are some guidelines that I recommend:

- If it doesn't need to be a conversation, send an email.
- If it is of an urgent nature outside of the school day, send a text.

- If you have a concern that you want to address, come with a solution.
- Never message your administrator on social media about things that are school-related.
- If you need something signed, drop it in their school mailbox.
- If you're expecting a parent to go to them, give them the heads up as soon as possible–especially if the parent is upset.
- If you make a mistake, tell them, and move on.
- If they seem short or dismissive with you, know that it's probably not about you. Something else is going on in the school that is occupying their attention. Don't take it personally.
- If they ask you to stop by their office at some point, do not assume the worst. They probably just remembered that they needed to talk to you and didn't want to forget.
- Always assume good intent.

When the Relationship Breaks Down

Inevitably, there may be times when the relationship with your administrator breaks down. My best advice is to remain professional, continue to do your job well, and communicate via email as much as possible.

There are many dynamics happening in schools, and it would be naive to think your relationships with colleagues will always be positive. That's just not realistic. It is most difficult, however, when it is your relationship with your administrator that breaks down, as they are in a supervisory role, which adds a different element.

If you feel comfortable doing so, you may want to consider addressing the situation head on. Ask your administrator if there is a time outside of the school day when you can meet and have a conversation.

When the time comes, use 'I statements' to share your feelings and understanding of the situation. Listen attentively when they speak and try to refrain from being defensive or reactive. Do your best to bring the situation to a resolution, but if that doesn't seem possible, try to at least end on a more positive note. You may also want to consider having someone else sit in the meeting, as well, to listen and keep the conversation on track if necessary.

Teacher Evaluations

I have yet to meet a teacher that looks forward to the teacher evaluation process. It adds another layer to an all-ready busy school year. For new teachers, it seems to cause a significant amount of stress.

While being evaluated may add some additional tasks to your school year, most evaluations go beautifully, and teachers are reassured by the feedback they receive. In the end, they realize that there was no need for the nervous anticipation and happy that another cycle is completed.

Potentially, during the evaluation process your principal may offer constructive criticism or suggestions for improvement. It may be difficult but try not to take their words too hard. Hopefully, they are also giving you positive feedback about your skills and celebrating the great things you do. Do not let the recommendations for improvement taint all the positives they have said as well.

Instead, take it as a learning opportunity and ask them for suggestions, resources, or even to demonstrate how to do what they are asking of you. Never let your administrator tell you that you need to do better at something without offering you the tools, strategies, and resources to do it. If they do not offer these things freely, ask for them. They are the instructional leaders of the school. It is their job to help you continuously get better at your job: teaching. It's okay to turn the question back to them and expect support.

Teacher evaluations are a part of the teaching process. They will happen continuously throughout your career. It helps to accept the process the best you can and know that it is a snapshot in time of what you do every day to meet the needs of students.

Final Thoughts

I have worked with many fabulous administrators over my twenty-five-year career in education. The best administrators never forget what it is like to be a teacher. And the exceptional ones never forget that we are all human with full lives beyond school.

Making a human connection with your principal and vice-principal is a great foundation for building a professional working relationship. Do not be intimidated by their title or role, and instead embrace their human nature.

ACTION STEPS

Here are some ways to begin building a strong working relationship with your administrators:

- Read all communications they send out to ensure you are not asking about something they have already addressed.

- Attend all staff meetings and address any questions or concerns regarding the information shared at that time (as long as appropriate).

- Determine when and how they prefer to communicate and do your best to follow suit unless there is a pressing matter or emergency.

- Always assume good intent but clarify immediately, if necessary.

- If you can get an answer from someone else, do it, and save the big things that no one else can help with for your administrator.
- Look for opportunities to invite them into your classroom to showcase student learning.
- Always engage with them on a human level first.

LESSON #6: Yes, it Is Nice to Have the Summers Off

Working in the Public Sector and Navigating Other People's Opinions

I cannot count the number of times over the past twenty-five years that someone has said to me, "Must be nice to get the summers off!" I've heard it from friends, family, and strangers. It seems that as soon as someone learns that you're a teacher, it's automatically where their mind goes.

Early in my career, I would attempt to respond and justify it. But I quickly learned that the best response is to say, "Yes, it is nice to have the summers off!".

Whether having "the summer off" is accurate or not, there is no sense in engaging in this type of conversation.

Each teacher's summer may look a little different, but as we know, most teachers spend significant time reading professionally, learning, taking courses, and just generally preparing for the upcoming school year.

The goal of this chapter is to address typical things that you might hear from non-teachers over the course of your career in education and prepare you for the impact that such statements may have on you. Adopting the correct mindset early on can prevent you from taking everything you hear personally and feeling as if you always need to respond.

That said, you will also experience words of support, encouragement, and empathy from others. Not all interactions with others will be challenging. Appreciate these positive interactions and use them as a reminder of the important work you do educating children.

What are Public Servants?

Most teachers are public servants. As public servants, we are government employees who are responsible for delivering the public service of educating children. Therefore, the government is our employer, and as such determines the education legislation, policies, and curriculum under which we work.

Working in the public sector means that politicians and political parties often use education to push their agendas, gain popularity, or discredit other politicians and political parties. During election cycles, these messages are often a focal point and can lead to even more questioning from people we encounter.

At times, being a public sector employee brings challenges.

How Does This Affect Me?

With the inundation of media sources and constant availability of such, these public messages can cause undue stress and uncertainty in the lives of teachers. This is particularly evident during contract negotiations and when funding is being determined for the next school year (especially for new teachers).

Many new teachers worry about job stability and whether

there will still be a teaching position for them the next school year. The ever-changing nature of the education landscape can be difficult to navigate, especially if you don't fully understand the process. While politicians are busy making political moves, the lives of thousands of teachers are affected.

Traditional Media

This messaging is further exacerbated by the media. The competition for readers and clicks is real. As a result, sensational or provocative attention-grabbing headlines are often used even when the actual article or news story may not negatively impact teachers themselves.

Some of this stems from politicians and political parties, but there are endless issues in education that can keep teachers, students, and schools at the forefront of the media year-round. Hearing and seeing these headlines everywhere we turn, over time, can create a constant sense of unease and often stress for teachers. This tends to peak during contract negotiations.

If you look for the silver linings, however, you just might find some.

During our last round of contract negotiations, the community I live in really rallied around teachers. Our local labor unions stood in solidarity with us and made their voices heard in the media. Our local restaurants and businesses donated food and services to teachers in a show of support, and community members and parents told us how much they valued what we do and that they were in support of our efforts.

During a stressful period for teachers, others came through. While it did not silence the messaging happening in the media, it perked us up and renewed our spirits.

Social Media

A different layer of stress can be found in the form of social media. On social media, everyone's an expert. Many people believe that because they've attended public school, they understand and can speak to education issues.

It is especially difficult when negative social media comments extend from family, friends, and acquaintances.

I have a family member that enjoys political debate. He brings up issues and comments on anything and everything that will spark debate. This is how he chooses to interact on social media. After reading his comments and positions on teachers, and education issues in general, I had to tell him that I needed to disconnect from him. And thankfully, he understood.

I needed to disconnect because I value him as a member of my family and respect that he gets to choose how he interacts within his social media platforms. However, I also knew that it would tarnish our relationship if I continued to read what he was saying about topics that are personal to me. For me, social media has a different purpose than what it does for him.

It is not only okay, but sometimes necessary, to set personal boundaries around social media use and who you choose to allow into your online space.

Social media can also be a breeding ground for misinformation as people often share what they see in other posts as fact without determining the accuracy of the information first.

Understanding What Is Happening and Correcting Misinformation

As a teacher, it is important that you have a reliable source for information for all things job-related. Having someone who can give you the facts and outline any potential impact it may have on your daily role is the only messaging you should listen to and is the only information that really matters.

It is essential that you have correct information and understand what is happening in the larger education sector, as well as how it may or may not impact you. Again, friends, family, and strangers will only know what they hear in the media and will believe it to be true since they have no other source. So, what will they do? They will continue to reiterate the information as true and factual whether it is or not.

There are two ways to proceed when you are presented with misinformation from someone outside of teaching. Either refuse to engage in the conversation or share facts with them and attempt to clear up the misconceptions.

There is no right way to proceed, and your choice will probably be different depending on the person you are interacting with. You may choose to correct misinformation with family or close friends and refuse to engage with others.

Either way, it is important that you understand the facts to the best of your ability and ask for clarification from trusted sources when you don't. There is much peace of mind to be gained from knowing the correct information yourself, even if you choose not to share it.

The Emotional Impact

There is no way to measure the emotional impact the "noise" in the media has on teachers. The impact tends to be somewhat of a continuum. I've seen it have a debilitating impact on some teachers and I've known others who can just brush it off.

Wherever you land on that continuum, it will most often impact you emotionally in some shape or form (even if it is just the fact that everyone around you seems to be constantly talking about it). It can also become exhausting to have others regularly trying to engage you in conversations about the latest news they heard.

You can actively protect your own mental health by adopting a healthy mindset and setting boundaries on your media consumption. The *noise* is not going to stop, so learning to manage it in a way that works for you is essential.

Lean on Your Teacher Friends

The good news is that you do not have to navigate it alone.

There are thousands of teachers enduring the same experiences as you. However, it is probably the teachers you are closest with that you can, and will, find comfort in.

If you need a moment to share your frustrations about what you are hearing or what people have said to you, teacher friends are the perfect listening ear. They can also be a great source for talking through how to respond to others, especially family members who you may not see eye to eye with, on topics around education.

As you gain more experience, you will develop your skills and preferences and will determine how best to navigate these scenarios.

The Other Noise

The other type of *noise* is more personal to the role of teachers than the larger education landscape, and that is when family and friends make comments toward you personally, saying things like:

"All you do is play with kids all day!"

"You only work six hours a day!"

"At least you don't have to work nights and weekends!"

"How hard can it be?"

"Teachers are greedy and always want more money."

My personal strategy when people make these comments is to, again, just agree. "Yes, it is nice to only work six hours every day" or "have weekends off" and so forth. And I usually add, "Don't be jealous!"

There really is no conversation to be had when someone approaches you with statements such as these. In my opinion, they are clearly looking for a reaction and trying to taunt you.

So, again, I encourage you to develop a strategy for handling these more personal comments since, I can assure you, they will never stop for as long as you are a teacher.

Final Thoughts

Try to find strength in the fact that there are so many teachers out there who do get your reality and understand the nature and scope of the work you do every day. Those are your people. Typically, teachers are a tight bunch. If you run into a stranger who tells you they are a teacher, you immediately gain a sense of comfort knowing that you are interacting with someone who gets it.

Other teachers are really the only ones who can fully understand, even better than your spouse, family, and close friends. So, fully embrace a circle of teacher friends to navigate the struggles and celebrate the wins with, as they can fully appreciate the magnitude of both.

ACTION STEPS

Here are some things you can do to actively prepare yourself for a career in the public sector:

- Find a trusted source to help you stay up-to-date and informed about things happening in education in your area.
- Adopt a mindset and strategy for navigating conversations with others that works for you.
- Actively protect your mental health.
- Limit social media use.

LESSON #7: The Only Constant in Education Is Change

Navigating the Swinging Pendulum as a Teacher

As you start your career in education, perhaps one of the most unexpected realities of teaching is the volume of change that you will encounter over the course of your career. If you're not a person who naturally embraces change, you will need to get comfortable with it quickly.

Most of this change is outside your control and will be thrust upon you as an expectation with a timeline. Just when you are hitting your groove and feeling comfortable with things, more change will happen. There are many reasons for this, including political changes, advancement in education research, cultural shifts, and funding, to name a few. Other changes may be the result of personal choice, such as a grade change or new school. Whatever the source, change is an inevitable part of a career in education.

Let's look at some of the more common sources of change that teachers experience.

Working and Learning Environment

Changes within your school environment most often occur at the beginning of the school year. However, there are factors which can lead to change at any point in the year. School districts are dynamic and continually evolving to offer the best services for students and their families. A change at any level can have ripple effects throughout the entire system. And other times, the impacts may be contained to only one school.

Administrator Changes

Principal and vice-principal changes can happen at any point in the school year. When they do, more than one school may be affected, as administrator changes tend to create a domino effect. It's important to note also that shifts in administration might occur several times during the same school year.

Administrators set the tone for a school and determine the specifics on how a school will run. As with teachers, no two administrators are the same. So, when a change happens, it often comes with changes from "how things are done" to how things are going to be moving forward.

Seasoned administrators will understand the importance of stability and consistency in a school and will generally not make any major changes mid-year. They opt instead to reserve significant changes for the start of the next school year. However, during your career you may encounter principals that will come in mid-year and turn things upside down.

Regardless of timing, all administrators will have their nuances as well as their own strengths and weaknesses. The skills of each new principal will have a significant impact on the school community and our daily work as teachers.

While everyone would like to work for administrators who are friendly, kind, and easy to get along with, perhaps more important to teachers is their ability to establish community and order; communicate in a timely and effective manner with staff, students, and parents; and cultivate a culture of support for their teaching staff.

Just as teachers have different personalities, teaching preferences, strengths, and weaknesses, so do administrators. It's best to approach a change in administration with patience, expecting that there will be changes and learning to adjust, as necessary, with the caveat that it is acceptable to advocate if you feel that the changes are not in the best interest of the school community, staff, or students. Sometimes, changes that are made don't make sense, and through gentle conversation with the new principal you can help them understand how what was already in place made sense and benefitted the school community. Seasoned principals typically welcome that feedback when it is presented respectfully.

Teaching Assignment

Another change that you will most likely encounter over the course of your career is a change in your teaching assignment. Often this may be a personal preference to either change grades, work in special education, or take on a leadership role such as an instructional coach. Other times, it could be a decision made by your administrator or due to a change of schools.

Whatever the reason, teachers tend to be creatures of habit who do not generally enjoy these changes because a change in teaching assignment often comes with learning a new role and new curriculum, which subsequently adds extra work hours to an already busy school day.

At the beginning of my career, I often hated change. I liked consistency and knowing what to expect, which might be why I spent my first nine years teaching grade three. However, after making a few changes in my teaching assignment throughout the years, I learned to embrace it. Changing grades, schools, or roles has a way of re-energizing you as a teacher. Suddenly, everything about teaching feels new and exciting again.

After nine years of teaching grade three, I made the change to become the teacher-librarian and prep provider. I was reluctant to let go of a homeroom because I thoroughly enjoyed it and thought that I wouldn't be able to develop the same relationships with my students when my class was changing every period.

To my surprise, I *was* able to build strong relationships with my students, and not only that, but I was able to build them with the entire student population. I also got to know our students well as readers and was able to engage them daily in conversations about books. How awesome is that?

I thought I was leaving my favorite grade and would never love anything as much as teaching grade three. Even though it was a welcome change, I still had my trepidations. In retrospect, I realized that I had become stale teaching the same grade for so long and no longer had the same excitement for the curriculum and learning opportunities I provided my students. It was the best decision I could have made for both myself and the students I was serving.

If I'd never taken the risk of making a change, I would have missed out on years of connecting with kids through books. Those years are among my fondest.

That said, there are pros and cons to a change in teaching assignment. The following chart explores a few of them.

Pros	Cons
• A new challenge often brings renewed energy and excitement	• Change brings new learning, which requires additional time
• Provides opportunity to explore what your strengths and preferences are	• May find that you do not enjoy your new assignment and it could take time to make another change
• Necessary step before pursuing leadership roles in the future	• Could lead to additional expenses for materials, resources, etc.

Class Makeup

A community's schools are each unique. No two communities are the same. When I was in elementary school, I had the same cohort of students in my class from kindergarten to grade eight. We spent nine years together and our families all knew each other.

As a teacher, I've worked in schools that are very transient. Students were constantly moving in and out of my classroom during the school year. From the class of students who I would begin with at the beginning of the year, maybe nine or ten were still there at the end of the school year. This happened repeatedly each school year.

Class makeup is one of those changes that we cannot control. As many veteran teachers can attest, one new student in your class has the potential to completely change your classroom dynamics (for better or worse).

> Relationships are the foundation of teaching and learning.

Relationships are the foundation of teaching and learning. It can be difficult for both teachers and students when children leave during the school year.

The Many Roles of a Teacher

Teachers are more than just educators to the students they serve. They are called upon daily to assume various roles to meet the needs of students and their families.

Teachers are often called upon to give parenting advice; be a listening ear; mediate friendships; support students through personal situations such as divorce, the death of a parent, or gender identity; assume the role of social worker, nurse, child advocate, coach, or mentor; or provide students with food, clothing, and other necessities.

Many veteran teachers have stories about ways that they have supported students that will both break your heart and inspire you. During your career, you will be called upon to be more than a teacher and this constant *changing of hats* can take an emotional toll over time.

Curriculum, Mandates, and Initiatives

Public education is an extension of the government, and as such, the government is responsible for setting the curriculum along with the policies, mandates, and initiatives that teachers are expected to implement and adhere to.

As education research and technologies (and society in general) continue to evolve, it is necessary to continuously reflect on curriculum standards to ensure that they are meeting the needs of our students and adequately preparing them for their future. Revisions are cyclical and typically focused on one subject at a time. This can make it feel like the curriculum is constantly changing when each new school year sees an updated version of subject-specific standards. One year it may be a new language curriculum, then the next year might be mathematics, and so forth.

Even when still teaching the same grade, the changes to curriculum can be extensive. This has the snowball effect of creating changes in our unit and lesson planning, resources, assessment tools, and so on. Sometimes it will even create a new learning area not previously seen in curriculum standards. An example of this is coding, which has only recently been added to curriculum.

As school districts attempt to digest and implement policies, mandates, and initiatives from the government, there will be many "for your action" items that are expected of teachers. And often, these items are expected to be used and fully implemented before any teacher training ever occurs or resources are provided.

Another catalyst for change is standardized testing. These test scores, which are a small snapshot of student learning in an artificial environment, are typically the impetus for targeted funding and policy by the government (which may or may not be the best focus for the long-term success of students). Yet, change will happen, and teachers will be expected to follow suit.

TEACHER TIP

Work at your own pace to make any changes that are mandated and refrain from imposing unrealistic timelines on yourself.

Research, Resources, and Best Practices

As education research continues to evolve, it drives changes and shifts in our pedagogy. Nowhere is this more apparent than with reading instruction. In the last fifty years we have seen the focus and practice of reading instruction shift from phonics to whole language to balanced literacy, and now to the Science of Reading.

With each new shift, things that were once "must-dos" get

thrown out and become restricted in favor of that which aligns with the new research (word walls get replaced with sound walls, leveled books get replaced with decodable readers, and so forth). We throw the baby out with the bath water at times, instead of trusting teachers to know when and how to continue to use these practices and resources.

> The frustration for many teachers is that the training comes well after the expectation to make the shift.

New research is followed with new best practices, new curriculum, new resources, new assessment tools, and eventually, new training. The frustration for many teachers is that the training comes well after the expectation to make the shift. This forces teachers to spend their own time researching and teaching themselves what they need to learn to make the necessary changes.

Learning Models and Technology

In addition to the research, models for learning continue to evolve. Recent models include flipped classrooms, inquiry-based learning, play-based learning, and cross-curricular, to name a few. Advancements in technologies also significantly impact our teaching and learning environments. With the speed with which these advancements happen, it is nearly impossible for our schools to keep up.

The wide availability of AI tools is challenging the way we not only do things, but how we assess student learning. While the initial reaction was to discourage and even penalize its use, education must accept these advances, and subsequent shifts in our practice, if we are to adequately prepare students for their future. However, these advances come with a steep learning curve for teachers.

My strategy with technology is to allow my students to "teach" me. What could take me hours to figure out on my own could often be learned by students in minutes. Technology has always been part of their world, and they have an innate ability to figure it out.

Once I've researched a platform and ensured that it is approved for use by my school district, I would give my students "free time" to play around with it and see what they discover. Typically, I allotted thirty to forty-five minutes for this discovery time and then we regrouped as a class and noted our findings together.

Things we would note:

- **The functions of the platform** – how does it work?

- **Best uses** – when and why would we use this platform?

- **Strengths and limitations** – what do we like about the platform and what are we not able to do that we wish we could?

- **Preferences** – would you use this platform or is there something similar that you find better?

This strategy helped me to not only learn the platform, but also to understand the potential uses for it and find out whether I had buy-in from my students. It served to develop their critical thinking around technology use, as well.

Special Education

Special education is another area where change occurs regularly. We are continually learning more about the brain and how it functions, about systemic barriers to learning, about early intervention, de-streaming, and many other areas that impact our special education policies and programs.

> The point on which we all agree is that there are not enough services in scope or availability to meet the needs of all learners.

I've worked in schools that have had self-contained special education classrooms as well as schools where students were fully integrated regardless of needs. Whichever model, current special education funding is not sufficient. The point on which we all agree is that there are not enough services in scope or availability to meet the needs of all learners.

Therefore, school systems continually apply Band-Aid solutions to special education, which often results in changes in personnel, services, supports, and resources, leaving teachers on the front line to fill in the gaps.

By giving 100 percent of what you have to give each day to your students, you are doing your part. You cannot fix a broken system, but you can serve children to the best of your ability given what you have to work with.

Change Fatigue

> With the constant inundation of change that teachers must endure; many inevitably experience change fatigue at some point in their career.

Change fatigue is a form of mental or emotional exhaustion that is caused by constantly needing to adapt to new situations, procedures, or expectations. With the constant inundation of change that teachers must endure; many inevitably experience change fatigue at some point in their career.

Teachers can become weary, indifferent, or even resistant to change when this occurs, which lowers both morale and productivity and often leads to burnout and high teacher turnover.

What exacerbates the situation is that, often, teachers are not consulted in the changes being made. These changes are being handed down from others who have never been the teacher in a classroom. This leaves teachers feeling devalued as professionals and disengaged from the process.

It is important to implement strategies that work for you personally to help avoid this fatigue that comes from the constant change in education.

Navigating Change

As a new teacher, you will need to learn to get comfortable with change. As the chapter title states: the only constant in education is change. If you are not naturally someone who embraces change, this may be hard at first, but will, hopefully, get better with time and practice.

Remember that you're not in this alone. You have a school full of professionals who are going through these changes with you. Connect with them, share frustrations, problem solve, and move forward together.

Strategies for Managing Change:

- **Get very clear on what you can and cannot control** — if you cannot control it, let it go and spend your time and efforts on what you can.
- **Never consider anything to be set in stone** — everything from class lists to teaching assignments, school personnel, resources, etc. Do your best to set yourself up to be ready to pivot if necessary.
- **Do not become attached to "things"** — things such as your classroom, resources, your supervision schedule, the "way things work" in your school, etc. It is okay to have preferences but avoid becoming attached.

- **Expect and anticipate change** — curriculum will continue to be revised, school districts will purchase new core resources and discontinue the use of others, technology will advance, etc. Always assume change is coming and be pleasantly surprised if it doesn't.
- **Set realistic timelines for yourself** — most change doesn't need to happen immediately. Set realistic goals and timelines, chunk the long-term goal down into manageable milestones, and collaborate with colleagues when appropriate to make less work for everyone.
- **Celebrate small wins** — take the time to reflect and appreciate when you handle change well or make progress toward new mandates. Share your small wins with other teachers who can appreciate your win for what it is.

When change happens, it's okay to be skeptical at first. It would be foolish to always jump into everything with both feet. So, if you recognize that something works for you and your students, it's okay to advocate for it to stay, or even to find a compromise between the change that is expected and the thing that is already working or successful.

> If we take the time to consider the thoughts, experiences, opinions, and expertise of others, we will arrive at what is best for the students we serve.

When change is on the horizon, it is important for all voices to be heard. If we take the time to consider the thoughts, experiences, opinions, and expertise of others, we will arrive at what is best for the students we serve. Make sure that your voice counts.

Final Thoughts

Change is hard. Whether welcome or not, it still has its challenges. Continuous change over an entire teaching career can take its toll. Do your best to find strategies that help you mitigate these factors and begin cultivating a strong teacher support group.

There is no end in sight to the ever-evolving education landscape. Learning to expect and anticipate change will help you to become more comfortable with it.

ACTION STEPS

Here are some things you can do to prepare yourself for and navigate the ongoing changes that happen regularly in education:

- Focus your energy on what you can control.
- Cultivate a mindset that embraces change.
- Ask questions and seek to understand why change is happening.
- Share your voice and opinions respectfully, as appropriate.
- Prioritize tasks and set realistic timelines for yourself.
- Seek help or support when needed.

LESSON #8: It's Your Job, Not Your Life

Establishing a Work / Life Balance

For many teachers, their job is a significant part of their identity. They take pride in the work that they do to help shape the lives of children and proudly tell others that they are a teacher. The knowledge and skills they develop from a career in teaching often filter into their personal lives, helping to form the way they live and interact with the world.

Teaching is not a job that is easily left at the door at the end of the school day. Worrying about students and losing sleep over the stressors of the role are commonplace. In addition, a teacher's entire workload does not fit into the school day, which forces most teachers to bring work home with them in the evening and on weekends. Trying to fit these work tasks into their personal time often leaves many teachers feeling like all they do is work.

Working in or near the community in which you live can

also make it hard to make the distinction between your personal and professional time. After teaching for a few years, many teachers become known in the community and will encounter both former and current students or parents when out shopping, dining, at community events, and so forth. Well-intentioned parents and students often engage teachers in school-related conversations during these non-working hours.

If you have children of your own, you also spend a significant amount of time supporting your own children's schooling. So, it's easy to see how teachers can feel that the line between personal and professional time is blurred.

In the Beginning

At the beginning of your career, you may think that this is just the way it is. This is what it means to be a teacher. And so, you run yourself ragged everyday trying to keep all the balls in the air and make yourself feel guilty about everything you didn't get to that day.

To try and ease the guilt and calm your anxiety, you spend even more time working. You start to sacrifice your personal time; your time with your family, friends or doing things you enjoy and become this person who is always working.

This Is Not Sustainable

While you may be able to keep this up for months or even years, at some point you realize that this is not sustainable. You are exhausted, your family is feeling neglected, and you can't remember the last time you did something just for fun.

At this point, you know something needs to change, but you don't see how you can lessen your workload. The guilt and anxiety about the impact this is having on those close to you starts to take over as the stress surmounts.

Learning to Let Go

This is when you need to have a good look in the mirror and

a long conversation with yourself. It is time to readjust your self-imposed standards of what it means to be a *good* teacher and take stock of your priorities.

Perhaps there are things at home that you can let go. Maybe you need to learn to be okay with an untidy house or cereal for dinner after a long day. But often, it's work-related tasks that need to be re-evaluated.

In a perfect world, every teacher would love to have a perfectly organized and decorated classroom environment, have all their lesson plans ready for the week ahead, be able to coach their favorite school sports, or would always invite parents into the classroom for special days.

Teachers are fantastic at making optional activities feel like must-dos because we love our jobs and the children we teach, and we can imagine all the great opportunities that we'd like to provide them. But the truth is you are only one person. Many of those *must-dos* in your mind are just preferences and things you'd like to do. Therefore, they can be omitted or altered to reduce your workload and recapture some of your valuable time.

I remember my first year at a new school. It was almost spring, and my students were asking me about our camping trip. Camping trip? They proceeded to tell me that the teacher before me (for more than a decade) always took her class camping for a weekend in May. They were super excited that it was finally their turn and they wanted to know the dates for *our* camping trip.

In talking to my colleagues, they all confirmed that this was the case and that I should be prepared for the parents to start asking me about it.

My mind was truly blown. How could this be an expectation? There was no way I was going to be able to take my class camping for an entire weekend with two toddlers at home. This was well beyond the scope of my responsibilities as a teacher.

Would I love to enjoy a weekend camping with my students? Of course. It wasn't about that. It was about one: the logistics of it, and two: the fact that it was just assumed that I was going to do it. It wasn't an ask; it was an expectation.

Now, I admit, this example is somewhat of an extreme. However, I still think it illustrates the point.

Real vs Perceived Expectations

Probably the most common "perceived expectation" that I think consumes many teachers is feeling like everything students produce needs to be marked or graded. That is simply not true. While it is necessary that we collect both summative and formative data on student progress, not every academic task needs a grade.

Sometimes it's just an opportunity for students to practice their skills. In these instances, they could self-evaluate their work, or you could provide feedback on their progress verbally. Occasionally, a learning opportunity *could* just be for fun.

Other things like coaching a team, running a club, helping with the breakfast program, or putting on a school play are also often *perceived expectations*. These are things that you may love to do (that are part of the reason why you became a teacher) but are not part of your job description. If you need to find more time or balance, it's okay to say no or refrain from doing these things when necessary.

I find that teaching tends to be cyclical when it comes to extracurriculars. Newer teachers tend to have less responsibilities outside of teaching, and therefore, more time and energy to commit to running many of the "extras" around a school. As life progresses, they may transition into family life where the demands on their personal time become greater. At this point, these teachers tend to slow down on their extracurricular commitments, allowing the new flock of teachers to take over. Once their families have grown, and as a more experienced educator, they begin to take on leadership roles within a school.

Schools generally have three sectors of teachers: those with a high commitment to extracurriculars, those being discerning with their "free" time, and others taking on the leadership roles in the school.

Obviously, this is not a hard and fast rule, but rather my observations over a twenty-five-year teaching career.

Setting Boundaries Around Your Working Hours

Another effective way to create more balance between your personal and professional life is to set boundaries. Start by determining your working hours. Typically, this would be the regular school hours plus some additional time either before or after school (or both), depending on your personal situation.

I am not a morning person and always preferred to stay after school to make sure that my loose ends were tidied up from the current school day and everything was ready to go for the next.

Creating boundaries also means setting a timeframe for your communications with parents and colleagues. Once you have left school for the day, it is important to disconnect from all methods of school-related communication. That means email, text messages, phone calls, and any school platforms.

Parents and colleagues will adjust and quickly learn your working schedule if you stick to it.

On the other hand, if you continue to answer school-related emails or call parents well after the school day, people will come to expect it. You get to decide your working hours outside of the school day and must train others accordingly. Make sure that your working hours are supporting your work-life balance.

Setting Boundaries Around Communication

Most school districts have platforms in place for school-related communication. Adhere to using the provided platforms to communicate with students, parents, and colleagues whenever possible. While it can be convenient to give a parent your phone number so that they can call or text you in that instant, you've then given them access to you twenty-four seven. You've somewhat lost control over your working hours when you choose to share personal access with others.

Similarly, I would suggest giving intentional thought to the social media platforms that you choose to participate in. Social media is an easy way for parents and students to find access to you during your personal time. A simple solution may be to use an alternative to your given name, making it less likely that you can be found. You can also change your settings to make things as private as possible.

At times, parents, students, or colleagues may not get in alignment with your communication preferences, and at that point you need to be prepared to have a conversation that's kind but firm. Reiterate your boundaries and ask them to respect your personal time.

Re-Establishing Your Priorities

Over the course of your career in education, the demands on your time will continue to evolve. You will gain more experience being a teacher, you may stay with the same grade for a prolonged period or take on a new role, your children will grow up, and your extracurricular involvement will change.

As such, it is important not to let yourself settle into "this is what I've always done" and instead continue to reevaluate your priorities and commitments at regular intervals (perhaps at the beginning of each new school year).

By doing this ahead of each school year, you can make conscious decisions about both your personal and professional commitments for the year rather than making rash decisions in the moment, which often leads to stress and overscheduling.

Each year may look different, and that's okay. Coaching the volleyball team last year doesn't automatically mean you need to coach it this year. Hosting family dinners for holidays does not mean you need to do every holiday. It's okay to continue to re-prioritize all aspects of your life so that it's manageable and has the balance that you both need and desire.

Prioritizing Your Physical and Mental Health

You cannot pour from an empty bucket. Taking care of and protecting your physical and mental health must, and should, always come first.

"I don't have any time for myself."

"I put on a school play *every* year."

"I *have* to write report cards."

I get it! Our natural reaction is to see all the roadblocks that stand in the way of doing what we need to do for our physical and mental health.

But I promise you, there is always a way to improve any situation or do what we need to do for ourselves. Instead of focusing on all the "yeah, buts," start thinking creatively, enlisting the help of others, learning about your school policies and protocols, whatever it takes. There is a way. You just need to figure out what it is.

Can I guarantee that your stressors will disappear? No. But I'm confident that you can find your way to a healthier situation.

As a teacher, I made it my mission to keep myself up-to-date and educated about our school district's policies and procedures, our collective agreement, and the mandates coming down from the Ministry of Education. By being informed, I was able to work them to my advantage when and if needed to prioritize my physical and mental health.

A Professional Example

If your school district's policy says that you must be informed thirty days in advance of a teacher evaluation, but your administrator tells you that they will be observing you next week, that does not need to happen. It is okay to advocate for yourself using the school district's policy and ask for a date with at least thirty days' notice. By doing so, you are relieving yourself of the undue stress of having to be prepared so quickly.

If your thoughts now turn to . . . I don't want my principal to be upset with me, or doesn't that look like I'm not prepared? . . . stop! None of it matters. What matters is your physical and mental health. Once you begin to set boundaries, others will adjust.

A Personal Example

Perhaps a significant date such as an anniversary or birthday falls during report card writing time. There is no rule saying that we can't celebrate these milestones on any date we choose. Instead of trying to tackle planning an extravagant party while writing report cards, simply move the date. Celebrate earlier or later, whichever makes sense

> for you. That doesn't mean you can't acknowledge the actual date in a smaller, more manageable way. It simply means doing the big celebration on a timeline that works better for you.
>
> Doing so will both allow you to write your report cards without distractions and enjoy every second of your big event.

Often, teachers have a significant amount of control over many of their personal and professional stressors. It's whether we choose to take that control that determines the outcome.

As a society, we need to stop glorifying being busy or overworked. It is okay to do nothing, and it is okay to put yourself first.

Taking Care of Yourself Makes You a Better Teacher

By making yourself a priority and establishing boundaries for your personal and professional life, you will become a happier, more productive, more effective teacher because you've taken the time to prioritize and focus on what is important to you.

Finding balance and happiness in your personal life allows you the mental capacity to give your best efforts to the students you serve. When your own personal needs are met, you are in a better position to meet the needs of your students.

Final Thoughts

Aiming to do all things at a high level is a lofty goal. As a teacher, it is great if you are driven and want to do all things to make your classroom and your school a fabulous environment for children. Schools need that level of enthusiasm and commitment.

However, the caveat comes when it is to the detriment of your physical or mental health. As a teacher, a friend, and a family member, you need to get comfortable with prioritizing your commitments and setting boundaries. It's not selfish, it's healthy.

Once you make this a habit, others will adjust and you will find more fulfillment in all that you do, both personally and professionally. Creating this habit takes time, but stay the course and remind yourself often of what's at stake if you don't.

ACTION STEPS

The following are some recommendations for steps you can take to begin to set boundaries and find a healthier balance between your personal and professional life:

- Determine your "working hours" and stick to them.

- Set up an auto-response in your work email for after-hours messages letting the sender know that you've received their email and will respond during your working hours, then state what they are.

- Take a hard look at both your personal and professional life and determine which things can be eliminated, delegated, or reduced.

- Think back to previous school years and make a list of the most stressful times of the year for you and identify the reasons why. What can you do to make them less stressful? Focus on the things you can control.

- Read and learn more about your school district's policies, your collective agreement, government legislation or mandates, or anything else that can help you understand and better navigate your working conditions and expectations.

- Identify areas where you view "perceived expectations" as must-dos and adjust as needed.
- Prioritize the personal and professional preferences that energize you, bring you joy, and are good for your physical and mental health.

LESSON #9: Teaching and Learning Are Supposed to Be Fun

Hitting Your Groove and Finding Joy in Education

Did you always want to be a teacher? Did you play teacher when you were younger? Or perhaps there was a crystalized moment when you decided you were going to be a teacher?

Whichever way your story goes, becoming a teacher isn't something that usually happens by accident. You don't just fall into the role of teacher. Typically, it comes from years of imagining being the teacher; longing to be a teacher. It is a passion within you that you must follow.

During my first week as a full-time contract teacher with my own classroom, I was standing at the front of the class teaching a math lesson. My students were engaged in trying a sample question on their own in their notebooks. I looked out at them from the front of the room and the moment just struck me. **I can't believe I am the teacher!** My thoughts and feelings in that moment overwhelmed me and the gravity of the situation just blew my mind.

It was a combination of realizing that I had fulfilled a life-long dream of becoming a teacher mixed with the overwhelming sense of responsibility I felt that their education was in my hands. **Like, I'm the teacher! How can I be the teacher?** I stood there for probably just a few seconds, but the emotion of that moment has stayed with me to this day.

Cultivating Your Mindset

As a new teacher, it is important to enter the profession with a healthy mindset; to acknowledge that this is going to be a huge learning curve and that it's going to be challenging. But also, that you are ready for this!

Take one day at a time, celebrate the small wins, and take comfort knowing that even the most brilliant teachers were once in your shoes.

Also remember that *you* get to set the tone for your classroom. Here are three things you can focus on to help you maintain the joy of being a teacher-even on the hard days.

1. Always remember why you became a teacher.

What was it about teaching that made you pursue it? Why did you want to be a teacher? Regularly recall the emotion and excitement you felt imagining the day that *you* would be the teacher!

2. Let your inner child out daily.

Build genuine connections with the children you teach and set a goal to make each school day a wonderful day for yourself and your students. Teaching may be one of the few professions where you can let your inner child shine daily at work (be silly, have fun, join in on games, sit on the carpet, play music, and so on). It's your classroom. You set the tone for the learning environment.

This isn't just for teachers of early years or primary classes. Older students love these things too. When you let your inner child out it gives them permission to put down their "cool persona" for a moment and just be in the moment with you. Whether they know it or not, and whether they'll admit it or not, even teenagers like and need this.

3. Create an environment that makes you happy.

Just like your home, your classroom should be a place you enjoy being. It should reflect your personality, your preferences, your style, and have some of the comforts that you enjoy. Whether that means decorating your classroom with a theme, having special pencils that are just yours, drinking your morning coffee from a fun mug, or creating a classroom-appropriate playlist to put on during the school day, integrate little things into your classroom that make you feel good and bring joy to the space.

These are just some of the things that you can do to set the tone for a great day of learning for both you and your students. These strategies can help you balance out the stresses of the job on the days when you need it most.

Teaching Is an Incredible Gift

As a teacher you understand that, for better or worse, you impact the lives of children. So, it is essential that you make every effort to ensure that you are having a positive impact on the students you teach.

As educators, we never truly know how our students experience us. We don't know whether we made a lasting impact or no impact at all, which students might carry things we've said or done into their future with them, or for which child we might be *the one* that made a difference.

Despite all of that, you can rest assured that you are making a lasting impression on the lives of children. This is both a huge responsibility and an incredible gift.

How lucky are we to play a role in the lives of so many children over the course of our career in education? If you can remember to approach each day accordingly and treat each day as the gift it truly is, you will be able to derive so much joy from your career.

> Imagine each child as the adult version of themselves, remembering the impact *you* made on their life as a child.

I challenge you to do your best to keep that thought at the forefront of all your interactions with the children you teach. Imagine each child as the adult version of themselves, remembering the impact *you* made on their life as a child.

Enjoy the Little Things Because They Really Are the Big Things

I would also encourage you to take the time to enjoy the little things. When a child draws you a picture or picks you flowers, when the teenager tells you you're cool or says thank you, when a parent feels better after a conversation with you, or your class performs at the school concert–these are the moments that matter most and will be remembered.

Curriculum is important. Learning is the main reason schools exist. However, it is these "other" things that will endure with you through a long, meaningful career. These moments will be the reason you persevere through the challenges of being a teacher.

I remember being at my first staff meeting as a new teacher.

A colleague was gifted with her twenty-five-year pin by our principal. At that moment, feeling the enormous weight of being a new teacher, I remember thinking: how can anyone do this for twenty-five years? I couldn't even fathom it. It just seemed so far away. Yet here I am, twenty-five years later. I cannot adequately express how quickly it flew by.

While there will be many long days, it really does feel like a short career when you get to the other side. Do your best to live in each moment and appreciate the little things that come with being a teacher. Like all things, it eventually comes to an end, and my hope for you is that you can look back with the fondest of memories and a sense of pride at all of the lives you touched.

Final Thoughts

While this book has covered a variety of topics and delved into some of the struggles and challenges of being a teacher, I can honestly say that I believe there is no better career.

It is important, though, to be intentional with your time, efforts, and energy. To make sure that you are driving the proverbial bus and that the bus (or the overwhelming nature of the role) is not driving you. Do your best to maintain your perspective, focus on the important things, and approach your role as a teacher with a healthy, positive mindset.

Teaching can and should be everything you ever dreamed of when you imagined becoming a teacher. Do not let others, the system, or the demands of the job steal that joy and excitement.

ACTION STEPS

Here are some ideas for starting your career well and finding joy in the work you do every day:

- Purposefully design a classroom environment that brings joy to you and your students.

- Add personal elements to your classroom that make you feel good such as photos, mugs, quotes, music, etc.
- Reflect often on why you became a teacher and what you hope to accomplish with a career in education.
- Intentionally celebrate the small wins each day.

LESSON #10: You've Got This

A Letter to New Teachers

Dear New Teacher,

Congratulations on embarking on this incredible journey as an educator! Your decision to become a teacher is a testament to your dedication, passion, and belief in the power of education to shape lives. As you step into your role, know that you are embarking on a path that will undoubtedly bring challenges, but also countless moments of inspiration, growth, and impact.

Remember, you have a unique ability to ignite the flames of curiosity and knowledge within your students. Your enthusiasm and energy will be contagious, and your influence will extend far beyond the classroom walls. Every lesson you teach, every interaction you have, and every relationship you build will leave a mark on the young minds entrusted to your care.

There will be days when you feel like you're not making

a difference or facing obstacles that seem insurmountable. In those moments, draw strength from your initial calling to this noble profession. Take a deep breath, remind yourself of your purpose, and remember that Rome wasn't built in a day. Every small step forward, every connection you make, and every smile you bring to your students' faces matters.

Embrace the journey of continuous learning. Teaching is an evolving craft, and each day offers new opportunities for you to refine your skills and discover innovative ways to engage and inspire your students. Seek out professional development, collaborate with your colleagues, and don't be afraid to ask for help when you need it.

Find your support network. Surround yourself with fellow educators who understand the challenges you face and can provide guidance, empathy, and a listening ear. Remember that you are not alone in this endeavor; a community of educators stands ready to uplift and support you.

Most importantly, take care of yourself. As you pour your heart and soul into your students, remember to replenish your own well-being. Self-care is not a luxury; it's a necessity. When you are at your best, you can better serve your students.

As you navigate this path, always keep your students' potential at the forefront of your mind. Your influence will help shape their future, instill a love for learning, and equip them with skills that extend far beyond the classroom.

Embrace the challenges, celebrate the victories, and cherish the small moments that remind you of the profound impact you have. You are embarking on a journey that will shape lives, and your dedication will leave a legacy.

Welcome to the world of education.

You've got this!

Acknowledgments

My awesome children, Myles & Kalen, for their patience throughout this process and for giving me the time and space to write a book!

My exceptional teacher friends for always cheering me on with their words of support and encouragement. I appreciate each one of you!

My amazing writing coaches, Geoffrey Berwind, Debby Englander, and Cristina Smith, for holding me accountable and whose knowledge, guidance, and support got me across the finish line!

My dedicated first readers, Megan Balsillie, Joseph Ferrarelli, Deb Demers-Hewitt, Michelle King, and Amy Soucie, whose time and feedback helped me write a better book!

My fantastic editor, Valerie Costa, whose expertise put the finishing touches on my manuscript!

My stellar book cover designer and formatter, Michelle Argyle Park with Melissa Williams Design, whose patience and tenacity brought my vision to life!

My brilliant photographer Heike Delmore, who made the experience an absolute blast!

A heartfelt thank you to everyone who helped bring my life-long dream of writing a book into reality.

teacherEDU Community

The teacherEDU Community is a place where new teachers connect, learn, and find support for the challenges that are unique to educators.

JOIN OUR COMMUNITY!

Use this QR code or **visit techeredu.ca** to become a member of our learning community today.

About the Author

After spending twenty-five years as an educator, special education specialist, and instructional coach, Shannon understands firsthand the realities of our current education system. Now she is on a mission to support, celebrate, and advocate for teachers while shining a light on the barriers they face in meeting the needs of their students.

Shannon also understands the unique challenges that new teachers face and is passionate about helping them to feel empowered and equipped for their role in education.

In 2023, Shannon founded teacherEDU, a learning community for new teachers. Through her private community and mentorship programs, Shannon offers new teachers the support they need, when they need it. You can learn more about her learning community at teacheredu.ca.

Shannon is available for speaking engagements and media/podcast interviews. To learn more about upcoming books, online programs or to contact Shannon, visit shannonhazel.com.

Shannon lives in Ontario, Canada, with her two children and dog, Rosco. She is enjoying her transition into life after teaching as an author, mentor, and advocate for teachers.

www.ingramcontent.com/pod-product-compliance
Lightning Source LLC
Chambersburg PA
CBHW050031040726

47599CB00015B/1629